Advance Praise for *Last Call*

"*Last Call* is more than a memoir; it is a manifesto of hope for those of us who have felt left out and left behind. This is not simply the story of Jerry's life from comedian to bartender to minister—it is a picture of what we are all called to: an unashamed, unrestrained, unrestricted expression of the life and love of God."
—Doug Pagitt, pastor and author of *Flipped*

"Jerry Herships reflects his own call to ministry: twisted, hilarious, and amazing. . . . Most of us do church in the tidy, comfortable confines of a church building. Not Jerry Herships. He's handing out the goods to drunks in bars and among the homeless in the park. Basically, my friend Jerry pastors in the exact places I'm pretty sure Jesus would be hanging out today. Let The Church—capital T, capital C— take note."
—Nadia Bolz-Weber, pastor and author of *Pastrix* and *Accidental Saints*

"I'm moved and inspired by Jerry's story and insights. Religion is a confusing and controversial institution that we humans tend to complicate. Jerry doesn't. Jerry is taking Jesus at his word. Love one another. Love your neighbor as yourself. Love yourself while you're at it. It's simple, but not easy. Even as a Jew, I see that if we followed the actual words of Jesus, we would live in such a joyous world."
—Mark L. Walberg, host of PBS's *Antiques Roadshow*

"Jerry Herships is a missionary, but not like you might think. Instead of trave~~ling overseas, Hership goes~~ to the bar and to the downt~~own~~ ~~something~~ that is more than just wor~~ds~~ from the world to the church. With his church, Jerry is conducting an experiment in ecclesial innovation, forming church where the people are gathered, making room for those who live somewhere between faith and doubt, and drawing focus to the simple practices of building community and feeding the hungry."

—Jeffrey Conklin-Miller, E. Stanley Jones
Assistant Professor of the Practice of Evangelism
and Christian Formation and Associate Dean for
Academic Programs, Duke Divinity School

"Jerry has a reputation around town as a healer of sorts. He's not the type that cures cancer with a single touch but the type that puts food in people's bodies so that they can survive another winter night in Denver sleeping on the cold, snowy streets. He offers the healing power of encouragement, an open ear, and hope. What Jerry does is truly inspirational. His story will motivate you to be better at life; to help others, to embrace the gift of love, and to drink more whiskey . . . judiciously."

—Ryan McDaniel, General Manager,
Don's Club Tavern, Denver

"Dorothy L. Sayers, a friend of C. S. Lewis, once commented, 'The people who hanged Christ . . . never accused him of being a bore—on the contrary, they thought him too dynamic to be safe. . . . We have efficiently pared the claws of the Lion of Judah, certified him 'meek and mild' and recommended him as a fitting household pet for pale curates and pious old ladies. Jerry does a superb job in sharpening up those radical claws again and removing Jesus from the boring subtleness of stained-glass windows. The church

needs to hear this biblical message and ask itself the question, am I willing to follow this wild, carefree God?"
—Gary Mason, Director, Rethinking Conflict,
and minister in Belfast, Northern Ireland

"I am an atheist. I don't believe in the 'God stuff'—I believe in the 'good stuff.' I believe that Jerry is and does the 'good stuff.'"
—Michele Smith, friend of Jerry Herships
and fan of AfterHours

"Drilling to the core of the gospel, Herships envisions a church as a collection of flawed individuals. . . . The church he describes has nothing to do with beliefs, budgets, or buildings; it is about doing the gospel. Herships is nothing less than a prophetic voice for our time."
—Jerry D. Campbell, President Emeritus,
Claremont Lincoln University

"*Last Call* is partly memoir, partly self-motivation gospel, and partly a call for a second Reformation. A raconteur extraordinaire, Jerry Herships narrates his story with humility, humor, and honesty and uses the lessons he has learned to offer a wholly new vision of 'church'—an inspiration for thinking differently about the future of Christianity in America."
—Pamela Eisenbaum, Professor of Biblical Studies
and Christian Origins, Iliff School of Theology

"In this raw and whimsical testimony I hear again and anew God's tug and nudge to tell the truth, to scoff at pretense, to live for others, to follow a path glimpsed only by the 'eye

of the heart.' This is a seer's oracle for a church seeking its way back to Jesus."
—Bishop Elaine J. W. Stanovsky, Mountain Sky Area
of The United Methodist Church

"Deeply personal and theologically timely. A moving memoir of personal transformation that illuminates the dignity of often-forgotten lives while raising essential questions about what the church sees as important."
—Thomas V. Wolfe, President and CEO,
Iliff School of Theology

"Jerry Herships is a rare leader in the church today. Somehow this former bartender and stand-up comedian has managed to plant a decentralized bar church for a denomination that for most of its existence has been officially dry. I still marvel at this one fact. But there is so much more. Earthy, at times profane in the manner of ancient prophets, Jerry calls the church to open its eyes and heart to all the possibilities of being the church beyond the confines of the usual buildings and programs."
—Elaine A. Heath, McCreless Professor of Evangelism,
Perkins School of Theology

LAST CALL

LAST CALL

From Serving Drinks to Serving Jesus

JERRY HERSHIPS

WESTMINSTER
JOHN KNOX PRESS
LOUISVILLE · KENTUCKY

© 2015 Jerry Herships

First edition
Published by Westminster John Knox Press
Louisville, Kentucky

15 16 17 18 19 20 21 22 23 24—10 9 8 7 6 5 4 3 2 1

Scripture quotations from the New Revised Standard Version of the Bible are copyright © 1989 by the Division of Christian Education of the National Council of the Churches of Christ in the U.S.A. and are used by permission.

Book design by Drew Stevens
Cover design by Barbara LeVan Fisher/levanfisherstudio.com

Library of Congress Cataloging-in-Publication Data

Herships, Jerry.
    Last call : from serving drinks to serving Jesus / Jerry Herships. — First edition.
        pages cm
    ISBN 978-0-664-26058-3 (alk. paper)
    1. Evangelistic work. 2. Drinking of alcoholic beverages—Religious aspects—Christianity. 3. Dinners and dining—Religious aspects—Christianity. 4. Non-church-affiliated people. 5. Church. I. Title.
    BV3793.H47 2015
    287'.6092—dc23
    [B]
                                                                    2015014674

∞ The paper used in this publication meets the minimum requirements of the American National Standard for Information Sciences— Permanence of Paper for Printed Library Materials, ANSI Z39.48-1992.

To Peggy and Ed, my mom and dad

My mom died the year I entered seminary, and my dad passed as I was finishing this book. I wouldn't have had a book to write if it hadn't been for them.

Thanks Mom and Dad. You taught me love.

CONTENTS

ACKNOWLEDGMENTS

This is the part of the book I was both looking forward to the most—and dreading. Looking forward to because it was so clear from day one that this was not going to be a solo endeavor. I like to give credit where credit is due. Dreading because I am relatively certain I will not find the words to express my gratitude to the people I mention here, or worse, that I will leave people out. My words are about to fall woefully short.

First, I would like to acknowledge all those who, like myself, feel they don't have it all together. The more I remember I don't have to have it all together, the happier I tend to be. So thank you to all the other people who feel like they are part of the Island of Misfit Toys. You make me feel not too alone.

To my wonderful wife, Laura. You told me to write a book for years. You thought I could do this *way* before I thought I could. Thank you. I think nine out of ten of us just want someone to believe in us. You believed in me.

To my son, Hudson, who heard night after night for weeks and months, "I'm going into the basement to write" and watched me disappear. As this book is published, you will be starting college. While I'm thrilled for you to be going off to college, I am happier about the man you have become. Thank you for allowing me time to write these words. You are funny, kind, and smart, and I am so proud of you.

To Pamela Eisenbaum, who might be the first person who believed these words could be a book. I will never forget the text you sent me that said you thought I had something here. I have such respect for you. You were the first person at seminary who made me feel like I was smart enough to be there.

To my amazing editor, Jessica Miller Kelley. You took a chance. I was already a writer (arguably). You made me an author. No one can take that away. I can't thank you enough. This thanks also extends to all the people at Westminster John Knox who went out on a limb by taking me on. You gave me a gift that no one else ever has or ever will. You gave me my first book.

To my good friend, Nadia Bolz-Weber. When I had nowhere to turn and didn't even know what I didn't know, you took my call—while you were in Turkey. Within minutes I was talking to Greg Daniels, who would later negotiate my contract (thanks, Greg!). Thanks for picking up your phone when most people wouldn't.

With every book there are tons of people that we never see. One of those with this book was my sister. While I was hunched over a laptop at the kitchen table or sequestered in my basement office writing these words, Joann cared for our father in the last year of his life. It was because she was doing that, that I could do this. Thank you, Joann. You are a saint.

To Bishop Elaine Stanovsky. If you and the cabinet hadn't been willing to go out on a limb and take a chance on something so weird, there simply wouldn't have been much of a book to write.

To Bill Barnes. If you hadn't seen something in me, I would probably still be leading "Name That Tune" and movie trivia during happy hour at some local bar. You saw something greater in me than I saw in myself. Thanks for not giving up.

To all my friends who took countless texts and calls as I was trying to figure out what the hell I was doing, who listened patiently and still stayed my friends. Thanks. You know who you are.

And lastly, to the community of AfterHours. You proved that my ridiculous dream of a different kind of church could be real. You and God made it happen. You're a good team. Keep that up.

INTRODUCTION
The Priest Club

I have been looking at this view for more than twenty years. In many ways, it has become a part of who I am.

I'm in my mother-in-law's den, overlooking Houghton Lake. It is the largest inland lake in Michigan. I have been coming up here every year for more than the length of my marriage, which as of this writing has been twenty-two years. It is one of the few places on the planet I can really relax and get perspective.

As I look on Carolyn's bookshelf, a book catches my eye: *Michigan Curiosities* by Colleen Burcar and Gene Taylor. It was the book my brother was writing when he died. He was 53. I'm 50.

When you "go home," things happen, whether you want them to or not. Your past collides with your future. You look for clues about where you are going next—if not the exact location, at least the direction. It is fitting that I am polishing up the last pages of this book here. I have returned to my past. It was at this desk overlooking the lake that I had the first discussion about AfterHours with key leaders back in 2011. I had a vision of a faith community where people could have a wider understanding of God and our relationship to him/her. I wanted to create a place where people could state what they believe and what they struggle with. Freely. I wanted a community of people who know we don't all have to agree on everything.

I looked out on the water, having no idea if what I envisioned could actually work, but I truly believed it would. I knew I would have to work hard to sell it, but I thought if I got the word out, it would help a lot of people reconnect to God.

Three years later, we've grown to hundreds of volunteers, handed out Communion to more than 50,000 people and lunches to more than 100,000, gained multiple corporate partnerships, gone from one location to four every month, watched as people redefined what church is, and watched people's lives change from either serving or being served. But I'm still not exactly sure who is changing whom.

AfterHours doesn't have it all figured out. It is just one way of connecting to God. I think it is a good way. It is one model that will connect with a lot of people who have not found a way to "do" church.

I myself knew how to "do" church.

I grew up Catholic in metro Detroit. Went to Catholic School, mass six days a week, and was an altar boy. Whole nine yards. I didn't think much about it (I was a little kid), but early on I encountered something that would stay with me my whole life: banana splits.

Father Szczesny was a retired Navy chaplain and served our parish for a short time. On Father Szczesny's birthday, he gave away coupons for free banana splits. Free! To a third-grader, this was the most amazing thing I had ever heard of. Not only was he not asking for presents on his birthday—he was giving out presents! This blew my little eight-year-old mind.

I had a great experience being an altar boy. No horrific stories, no awful memories. Except that my altar boy career almost ended before it even began. I damn near lit the church on fire within the first five minutes of mass.

It was my first time coming down the aisle as an altar boy, and I was to carry the candle-on-a-stick thing. (I'm sure it had a better name, but whatever.) It was going swimmingly well the whole way down the aisle: no tripping, no dripping, candle stayed upright, perfect. I even kept pace with the priest (harder than you would think; he would almost sprint going down that aisle). It was going great.

It wasn't till I had to actually get the candle *into* the candleholder that we ran into trouble. The base was old, and you had to jiggle the candle-on-a-stick to get it to go in. I must have missed that meeting. As I tried to force the candle-on-a-stick into the base, I came to the realization that everyone else was done and all eyes were on me. This didn't help. Finally, after much sweating, I was able to get it on the base, and it went in with great force—so much so that the heavy brass cap that was on the top of the candle flew off and went sailing across the front of the church. I chased after it, and after retrieving it, I put it back on top of the candle (which was now out with no way to relight it).

As I slowly took my seat and the adrenaline stopped, I realized just how embarrassed I was. I could feel hot tears slowly rolling down my face, which made me *more* embarrassed. It was hard to stop the tears but I dared not try to wipe them away, as that would cause even more attention. Mortified, I saw my altar boy career pass in front of my eyes.

In a moment of great compassion, I saw the priest lean over to the head altar boy and whisper something in his ear. He turned and whispered to the second-in-command. (I don't technically know if there was a second-in-command, but I knew I was on the bottom of the pecking order.) The second-in-command leaned over and whispered in my ear,

"Father says if you're gonna cry, go in back." (This is what we in the business call "pastoral care.") I went in the back and cried.

This was my introduction to formal ministry.

Despite this, I pressed on. I enjoyed spending time with the other altar boys and hearing all I could about the church and the priest's life. At this early age I got bit and got the bug.

I wanted to be a priest.

I assumed at this juncture that I couldn't possibly be alone, so I approached my third-grade teacher, Sister Mary Ann. Sister Mary Ann was, as my dad was prone to say, a tough broad. (And my dad knew about tough sisters. He was raised by the priests and nuns at a boarding school in Canada from the time he was in third grade through twelfth. I can't imagine.)

Sister Mary Ann asked me what I wanted. I asked her if I could stay after class to ask her a question. I was scared to death. (Once I saw her pick up a desk and hold it up over her head to empty everything out from under the seat because it was messy. Like my dad said—tough broad.) I told her about my desire to become a priest. Her look softened, just for a second, and then she asked what I needed from her. So I told her.

"Well, I figured if I want to be a priest, others must want to be a priest too. So I wanted to see if I could start a Priest Club after school." She just stared at me. Then she said music to my ears: "If that is what you want, let's do it." I was so happy. For the next four weeks, I was allowed to go around to the other classrooms and announce, "Hi, everyone. My name is Jerry Herships. I want to be a priest. If you want to be a priest too, meet me in Sister Mary Ann's room after school and we'll talk about Priest

Club stuff." I had no idea what "Priest Club stuff" was. I just knew there had to be some kind of stuff to talk about. For four weeks, I made the rounds, and for four weeks, I showed up after school.

No one came. Ever. Not once.

And that was my first attempt at trying to start a faith community.

Between breaking down in my first mass and logging a zero for attendance in the Priest Club, it wasn't looking good. (Plus Father Szczesny told me I had to read the Bible and I couldn't get married. I already liked girls.) This was bad news all the way around.

I didn't entertain the idea of ministry again for thirty-two more years. I was a late bloomer.

At one time, I had bigger dreams than anyone I know—and they were crushed. I was going to be big—big enough that all those years tending bar to make ends meet would be just a funny sidenote in my Emmy Award acceptance speech. When those dreams came crashing down, I heard God calling me to ministry—a whisper in the rubble.

I barely got through seminary. I worked for my denomination's biggest church in a five-state region one day, and the very smallest the next. I find myself getting pissed off at the church more days than not. I heard someone say once that the good news is that 100 million people go to church on Sunday, and the bad news is that 200 million people don't. Here's the real kicker: I am not convinced God cares.

Over the last ten years I've realized a few things.

1. Jesus never said, "Sing and pray and tell me I'm great once a week." Can't find it. I've looked.

2. Jesus *did* say, "Do as I do," "Feed my sheep," "Go now and do the same," "Love one another as I have loved you."
3. There are more than four hundred verses that ask us to care for the poor. I think this was a major talking point for the Good Book. God wants us to get this one. If highlighters had been around then, I think he would have used them on those passages.
4. It is easier for everyone, clergy and congregations, to put on great events on Sunday than it is to go out and care for the poor.
5. All these comments tend to really piss off people who go to church.
6. These comments never piss off those who don't go to church and are often listed as among the main reasons they don't.

I think it's ironic that the more I talk to people outside the church, the more I realize they are just looking for something bigger than themselves. They want community and a way to serve the world and give back. They could not care less about our preaching, hymns, and fancy buildings. Declining church attendance and numerous polls are evidence that support this.

The very thing people want is (ironically, perhaps) the very thing Jesus told us to give them: Serve and love others. Create community. Follow Jesus. Instead, we give them boring sermons, music they don't know (and don't *want* to know), and—wait for it—building campaigns.

And we wonder why no one shows up.

Not only are we not giving them what they want, but I don't think we are giving them what Jesus wants.

By most conservative measurements, I am a heretic. No question. They thought Jesus was too. And that's why I got into ministry. I was told a long time ago that there was only one way to do the God thing and if you didn't like it not to let the door hit you in the ass on the way out.

I didn't let it. I left the church for nearly ten years. Never set foot in one.

When I found out there were a lot of ways to connect to God, my first thought was, "Does anyone else know about this?" I was pissed.

Looking for people who were actually talking about these other ways of thinking, I enrolled in seminary. There (and in many conversations since), I've learned that most pastors are actually more progressive than we think. Most of them don't say what they really think in regard to hell or gay marriage or the Virgin Birth, or even their own struggles with depression or addiction, because they are afraid they will lose their flock—and a ton of money.

To hell with that.

Chapter 1

BRIGHT LIGHTS, SMALL CITY

A thousand people a show, six shows a day, five days a week. Twelve shows on Saturdays. That's forty-two shows a week. Forty-two thousand people a week. For two summers. That was my first professional job as an entertainer. I performed in front of more than a million people *before* I moved to L.A.

And on top of that, I met the woman I wanted to spend the rest of my life with. Twenty-eight years in, I still do.

Now *that* was a good job.

Cedar Point in Sandusky, Ohio, is one of the oldest and most successful amusement parks in the country. It is famous for its roller coasters and at the time also had a strong reputation for its live shows, of which there were more than half a dozen throughout the park—none of which used recorded music.

I performed there for two summers in the IMAX theater. I was actually part of the preshow before the IMAX theater show. We were in the covered but still outdoor theater attached to the indoor movie theater. There were doors at the end of every row, and the people in our theater would just stand up, walk down their row, go through their door, sit down inside, and watch their movie. The rumor was that the theater designers consulted with the military on how to move a large number of people. That always struck me as odd, unless there is some division of the armed forces that specializes in watching films. At any rate, ten minutes after the house was loaded I would do a fifteen-minute comedy show highlighting things to see in the park. At the end, the doors would open, the guests would file into the IMAX theater, and I would relax for about fifteen minutes till we opened the house and did it all again.

I got to do the forty-two shows a week for $210 a week. I thought I had died and gone to heaven. I still don't know when I have had that much money and those few cares.

The show that I did every day, day in and day out, was unbelievable training for my future years. I learned how to handle almost every kind of situation, including performances where the rain was coming in *sideways* and I was still on stage, convinced I would be electrocuted. It was work, but I had a ball. I loved it so much in 1985 that I went back in 1987.

It was the one time in my life when I dated a number of people, especially when I first got there. (The unofficial slogan of Cedar Point's mainly college-aged employees was "When the park closes, the rides don't stop.") I was a little more reserved than that, but it was still a fun summer. When I went back to school that fall at Western Michigan University, I was ready to keep my dating life alive and well.

I could not find a girl to save my life. Nothing. Nada. Not a single date.

I learned something that stuck with me for a long time: At Cedar Point, people were not dating me; they were dating my job. Although it was as small a pond as you could have, I was still a big fish; working in the "entertainment department" and having a one-man show carried some cache, as silly as that sounds. It was my first exposure to the power of "celebrity," even in Sandusky, Ohio. It was a hard lesson to learn.

When I went back two summers later, it was different. I was months away from pursuing my dream. I couldn't be distracted. I was driven and laser focused. There was a singer/dancer in one of the other shows that every guy had their eye on. A tall, leggy redhead named Laura Ballard, she was not very interested in "dating around." I was getting ready to leave for L.A. at the end of the summer to take over *The Tonight Show* (at least that was the plan) and had no interest in being tied down with a girl. After hanging out as friends, we started hanging out, well, more. We thought it would be perfect; I could be her "date" to things so that other guys wouldn't bother her and I wouldn't have to worry about getting attached to a "girlfriend." Whew! Sure glad we had that all figured out.

Laura and I had an amazingly romantic summer, but I was determined to move to L.A. When I went to leave that morning in October, she was there to say good-bye. I drove away and didn't think about her again . . .

. . . till about Lincoln, Nebraska. I remember calling her that first night away, just to "check in," no big deal. I remember saying, "Hey, it's Jerry." She responded with, "Jerry? Jerry? I know the name." Funny girl.

Five years later we were married.

Anyone who tells you that marriage is easy is either lying or single. Anything worth it, especially if it's long term, is hard. So? Those are the things in life that are worth it. I have still to this day never met anyone else I want to spend the rest of my life with.

And she has put up with the ultimate switcharoo. I told her I was going to be a comic, and then a game show host, and then a talk show host, and then the day would come when I would take over *The Tonight Show*. (I could prove it because I had it all written down on a piece of paper with one-, five-, ten-, and twenty-year goals—in *pen!* I was not kidding around.) Twenty years later, we were in Denver. I was graduating from *seminary*, working in a church, preaching, and starting to spend time with drug dealers, junkies, homeless folks, and hookers (okay, that last part was a lot like L.A., but the rest . . .). I totally pulled a bait and switch. She thought she was marrying Johnny Carson. She ended up with Billy Graham. I didn't mean to. But at some point, I started listening to God's plan, not mine. God didn't even write it down!

LIVING WITHOUT FEAR

"Never, never, never give up." This is a famous Churchill quote. It was also my mantra for all those years in L.A. and beyond. I simply refused to quit. Maybe that's your mantra now too. We are a society that applauds stick-to-it-iveness. Tenacity is always revered. The problem is that this same desire to not give up can blind us to other opportunities that are opening up around us. Designer Paul Smith wanted to be a professional cyclist before an accident laid him up in bed. During his recovery, he picked up a sketch pad. Billy Crystal always wanted to play professional baseball for the Mets. He decided to do comedy instead after watching his other dream die. Jack White of the White Stripes was a drummer till he formed an early band with a friend who was also a drummer, so he picked up a guitar.

What kind of opportunities could you be missing right now because you are scared to quit the old dreams and move on to new ones? Maybe it is just a matter of redirection: making a slight tweak here or a small change there. It takes bravery to stick to your dreams regardless of outcome. It also takes courage to evaluate where you are and to adjust your sails when the winds change.

I have a tattoo that says *sine metu*, which is Latin for "without fear." I think fear is the opposite of love and that fear is what holds us back most of the time. What I *didn't* know until a bartender pointed it out to me is that *sine metu* is also on the family crest of Jameson Irish Whiskey. If I have to have something written on my arm that's also on a bottle of booze, it beats Goldschlager.

I think learning to live into who we are is one of those things that is easier said than done. One of the biggest victories of getting a tattoo in the first place was being able to squelch the voice in my head that said, "What will people think?" Those four words are poisonous. They have kept more people from singing karaoke and dancing like a fool than almost any other thing. We become so consumed with what people think that we stand paralyzed on the sidelines, never getting into the game of life. Sadly, I think this kind of fear affects most of us.

It isn't easy to let people see the crappy stuff in your life, the demons you've been fighting for years and just can't beat, or just the quirks you'd rather hide. For me, it's my obsession with my weight, my vanity, my ego, and my addiction to Diet Coke. It's ugly stuff.

There has not been a day in the last four decades when I didn't think about how many calories I was putting in my mouth. From third grade on, I knew I was "the fat kid." It has shaped and formed my self-understanding and self-image ever since. I was the kid who *always* ate two Burger King Whoppers (with cheese, minus pickles). My family would say, "Give it to Jerry, he'll eat it." And I did.

I have yo-yoed my whole life. In the last year alone, I weighed 190 at one point and am now up to 215. Three years ago I was at 230.

The irony is that I preach about loving yourself the way God loves you: without judgment, without qualification, without condition.

Physician, heal thyself.

I do think we are called to love ourselves. Jesus said to "love your neighbor as yourself." That assumes we love ourselves and shows that loving ourselves is a prerequisite for loving anybody else!

I think if I had one wish for the world, it would be self-love—not the one-handed kind, but real self-*love*. A love where we forgive ourselves more quickly. A love where we *know* we are train wrecks but that's okay. A love where we accept ourselves when we have love handles or have a keg for a stomach instead of a six-pack.

We need better self-talk. We need to talk to ourselves and think about ourselves the way Jesus thinks of us—as if each of us is the most awesome person he knows. The thing is, it's a tie. Everyone is exactly that awesome. It's the best kind of tie.

We need to know that Jesus loves us unconditionally, imperfect as we are. And when we have the courage to show the world our imperfections, we find that others will show us theirs as well, and we can limp along the road together. It is always an easier journey with someone next to you. You can find a way back to yourself, to be fully who *you* were meant to be—complete with foibles, tattoos, and love handles.

This is the brilliance of AA or any of the 12-step programs. Before anything else, there is an admission: "I'm
an alcoholic." That is a no-bullshit statement right there,
claiming your stuff. I have had people say to me that keeping the secret is harder than the addiction itself. I believe it.

If I get another tattoo (we'll see), it will be the words
"To be nobody but yourself," part of a quote by ee cummings: "To be nobody-but-yourself—in a world which is
doing its best, night and day, to make you everybody else—
means to fight the hardest battle any human being can fight;
and never stop fighting."

And make no mistake—it's a battle. It is a constant
contest to see if the voice saying, "Do you know what people will think if . . . ?" will win. This voice keeps you from
singing and dancing and writing and ordering dessert and
getting a tattoo and . . . You have to shut that voice down—
every single time.

By the way, sometimes you will still get the shit
kicked out of you. So what? Get up, curse, cry if you have
to, *and try again.*

This kind of living will make you an outsider. In the
words of Thoreau, "The mass of men lead lives of quiet
desperation." Most of us are cowards and are comfortable
living life in the theater seats rather than being on stage in
the play. Getting out there and facing the fear, trying again
and again, will get you labeled unique or different or just
weird. And it's lonely—*until* your idea catches on. Then
people will label you (as they did throughout history to
those who did the same thing) "innovative," "brilliant,"
"creative," or "genius." The irony is that *anyone* can reach
this point if they are willing to take the slings and arrows of
being different in the early years. I have been unique and

different and have marched to my own drummer my whole life. I am far from these labels, but at least I am beginning to get used to being different. I am getting more comfortable with the idea.

Whatever it is you're dreaming and planning and trying to be, be nobody but yourself.

Chapter 2
BRIGHT LIGHTS, BIG CITY

People always say Hollywood's a tough town. It's hard to make it. You can get fired at a moment's notice and get replaced, and they use people up like Kleenex.

Well, that's true.

But there is a lot of good, too. Unfortunately, this is not one of those stories. This is about how I got and lost my first Hollywood gig within thirty days of living in L.A.

I moved to Los Angeles with someone I barely knew, and he has since become one of my oldest and dearest friends. Steve Davis and I drove cross-country from Detroit to L.A. to find our fortune. (We still have outstanding warrants for speeding tickets we both got in Lincoln, Nebraska. To this day, I always feel a bit like I'm on the lam whenever my travels take me through Lincoln.)

Steve's plan was to be the next Steven Spielberg, and I was going to be the next Johnny Carson. Steve is still out there and has made a living in entertainment since day one, except for one small stint as a soda jerk that he can share in his own book.

When we got to L.A., Steve had arranged for us to live with his cousin Leonard in Beverly Hills until we could get our feet on the ground. And if we never got our feet on the ground, at least we'd be living in Beverly Hills! (If I remember right, we only lasted about two weeks with

Cousin Leonard. Steve says he still asks about me. I can only assume I owe him money.)

As soon as we arrived, the houseboy grabbed our luggage and took it to an undisclosed location (there were not a lot of houseboys in Detroit, at least that I knew of, so this was very cosmopolitan to me), and Leonard told us to get ready for a small dinner party he was throwing in our honor.

There were about fifteen people at the party, all Hollywood-type folk. (Leonard was Richard Dawson's manager and, as a result, knew everyone.) One of the people at the party was a man named Arthur Annecharico, who ran a production company called, aptly enough, the Arthur Company. (They saved the creativity for the shows.) The company was just getting ready to begin working on a show called *The Munsters Today*, which was a remake of the hit series from the 1960s. This new series had the distinction of being the only show I know of that had Dr. Joyce Brothers, Zsa Zsa Gabor, and Norman Fell as guest stars.

The woman seated to my left at the dinner was Arthur Annecharico's wife, who asked me, "So what do you do?" I told her I was a host and emcee and comedian. She turned to her husband, Arthur, and said, "Have you found a warm-up for *The Munsters Today* yet?" He said no, and she turned to me and said, "Call Kim Dorr and tell her I told you to do so." I had a job as the warm-up comic for *The Munsters Today* the very next week.

Apparently, it *is* who you know.

It is worth noting that at the dinner I had absolutely _no_ idea what a warm-up comic was. I learned quickly that the warm-up comic was the guy who entertained the studio audience when the show wasn't taping. You could do this however you wanted, but generally, it had to include funny.

You could do sing-alongs, tell jokes, do trivia, whatever—as long as it was funny. At this point I had about fifteen to twenty minutes of solid material. A taping for a 22-minute show generally took about three to four hours, depending on wardrobe, set changes, etc. If your math is as good as mine, you will have figured out that I was coming up about two hours and eighteen minutes short of material.

I learned quickly.

A couple of weeks into the job, I mispronounced the name of one of the lead actors during the taping. Barely. I got a call two days later from the show's casting director, Kim Dorr. "We have a problem," she said. "Let's fix it," I responded. "I don't think we can," she told me. "One of the stars didn't like that you mispronounced their name. They want you gone, and even though I think you're great, the star rules."

I got my first job in Hollywood within my first week. I got fired from my first job in Hollywood during my third week.

I called my brother with the words "You will never work in this town again" playing over and over in my head.

In Gene's classic way of setting things right, he said, "Wait. If the worst thing that ever happens to you in Hollywood is that you got fired from *The Munsters Today*, you are going to be just fine." He was right.

What that particular experience taught me was what a spoiled little bitch I was. Gene, in his wisdom, reminded me of three words: perspective, perspective, perspective. If I looked at the glass as half-full, I already landed my first job in Hollywood *and* had been fired! It was nowhere but up from here.

My brother Gene was the producer and head writer for the number-one morning radio show in Detroit, *The Dick Purtan Show*. Gene had hosted a number of television shows in Toronto and had been a writer and performer all his life.

I wanted to be like him.

It is a relatively safe bet to say I probably never would have gone into show business if it hadn't been for Gene. Like most younger brothers, I looked up to him and tried to copy him. To this day, he is the only guy I ever knew that liked clothes as much as I do. He wore bow ties to work every day except on casual Friday. Then he wore an ascot.

Gene died young, the result of a bad asthma attack at age 53.

Too many times we lose sight of just how great we have it. I was pursuing my dream in L.-freakin'-A.! I had a great roommate, a great family back home, and, oh yeah, I was living in Beverly Hills!

Life was pretty damn good. But that doesn't mean it was easy.

AUDITIONING ON THE ROOF ON SUNSET

One of the hellish parts of trying to make it in comedy in Los Angeles is if you are out there trying, everybody already knows how bad you want it. *You moved across the country for it!* As a result, the humiliation factor can go way up.

Fortunately, humiliation was not new for me. One of my first jobs back in Detroit was as a fully costumed village barkeep. I have bartended a big chunk of my life. I had to start somewhere. Everyone does.

I started in the 1800s.

My first ever bartending gig was working in an 1800s tavern in Greenfield Village in Detroit. Greenfield Village was attached to the Henry Ford Museum, a car museum that, incidentally, was and still is amazing. Go if you get the chance. I think they have both the bus on which Rosa Parks made her stand for justice and the Oscar Mayer Wienermobile. Not every museum can make that claim.

Greenfield Village was supposed to recreate what a real village would have been like in the 1800s. What this has to do with cars I have no idea. If you grew up in Detroit, you just always put them together. We never questioned it. It wasn't till years later that I started to wonder what the rationale was to put hot rods from the 1950s next to a blacksmith's workshop. Regardless, it was what it was, and to this day it's a ragingly popular museum.

I was not a blacksmith. I like to believe I was one notch above the blacksmith. As the bartender in the village tavern, I wore ridiculous brown baggy pants, a blousy cream-colored shirt that looked vaguely like a pirate shirt, and a gigantic brown floppy tie that I knotted in a bow. Despite the reputation of bartenders (half the reason you get into this line of work), there was no way I was going to get laid.

We were not allowed to serve anything that didn't exist in the nineteenth century. This effectively kept me from having to serve Ye Olde Long Island Iced Tea, or the Village Irish Car Bomb. It also eliminated vodka. We served some messed up drinks.

I remember having to mix industrial-size packets of light greenish-yellow powder into huge buckets with water that would later be the base of one of our old fashioned(ish) drinks. I didn't even know they had powdered juice packs in the 1800s. I would often end up sticky and smelling kind of like Country Time lemonade. *Cocktail* this was not, and there was no way in hell I was Tom Cruise.

But it did what it was supposed to do: it allowed me to put "bartender" on my resume and to do it honestly.

I remember reading about Eddie Murphy telling Chris Rock that you can't be funny and cool at the same time. You've got to choose. Tell that to any young comic trying to land a stage, any stage, anywhere in L.A. You're trying to be funny enough to get the laugh and cool enough not to be laughed off the stage. In the beginning, you aren't even trying to get jobs; you are just trying to get stage time so you can learn not to suck and *get* good enough to actually *look* for work. You can't practice comedy on your own. It's not like practicing the tuba. The audience is the only barometer for whether you are improving or not. All other arts have rules and specific guidelines. Comedy does not. There is only one barometer of success: Did they laugh? And in order to know for sure, you need a "they." Open mic nights were everywhere in the late 1980s. Not only were there lots of clubs, but there was a comedy night at almost every bar in the city. You just went around driving from open mic to open mic. You did your three to five minutes, got off the stage, walked out with your tape recorder, and went to the next club. (Kids, tape recorders were these devices that—actually, just Google it.) Getting stage time was huge in helping you hone your act. Doing it in front of a mirror at home in your crappy bathroom with the paint coming off the walls wasn't gonna cut it. You needed warm bodies. And not in your bathroom.

This is why landing an emcee gig was so important. It gave you guaranteed time to work on your craft. I know how pretentious "craft" sounds, but comics really do think of what they do as art. It might not seem like art to you, but it is—like poetry or writing. In fact, it is poetry and writing.

Emceeing was so important in L.A. that there was a lot of competition to land these jobs. While any stage was good, there were stages that were higher up the ladder than others. The Comedy Store and the Improv were the two big ones, but there was also the Hermosa Beach Comedy and Magic Club and the Laugh Factory. Hermosa Beach was where Jay Leno worked out his material for *The Tonight Show* when he was filling in for Johnny Carson on Monday nights. He felt the crowds were a little bit more like the heartland than the jaded crowds at the Comedy Store or the Improv (assuming that the heartland lived by the beach on some of the most expensive real estate in the world, and was stunningly good looking and blonde.)

The Laugh Factory opened in 1979 and wasn't even ten years old when I was trying to land stage time there. Already it had an awesome reputation and was located right on Sunset. To land a gig there would be fantastic. (You may remember the Laugh Factory as the club where *Seinfeld's* Michael Richards had his comedic meltdown a few years back.)

As luck would have it, I had heard about the club holding auditions for a house emcee. (Comedy clubs rarely posted things; you just had to kind of "hear about" them.) I arrived at the club and was one of probably ten or twelve. There was construction going on in the club, and it would have been impossible for the comics to audition on the stage with all the noise. After talking to each of us for a few minutes, the guy in charge picked six of us to audition for the emcee job and told us to follow him upstairs.

We climbed the stairs to the second floor where the offices were. I assumed this would be where we would do our audition. There were one or two other people at desks on phones, and it occurred to me that this would be an equally awful place to do an audition. I think the guy running the audition came to the same conclusion when he said, "Hang on. I've got an idea. Follow me."

He led us to a circular staircase, and we started climbing. At the top, we opened the door and found our audition location.

We were on the roof.

He told us, "Here's what I want you to do. Pretend you are introducing a guy named Mike Roberts. He has been on *Late Night with David Letterman* and *The Tonight Show* and has performed all over the country. Show me how you would introduce him." I asked him if he wanted to hear any of our material. "No," he said. "Just do an intro for this imaginary comic." We were standing on a rooftop covered in gravel, with cars driving by below on Sunset and the L.A. skyline strung out in front of us. It would've been beautiful if it hadn't been so ridiculous and humiliating. One by one, we separated ourselves from the others, then turned around and faced them—the guy running the audition plus half a dozen other comics that hated you and wanted you to screw up and, with any luck, fall off the roof.

When my turn came, I walked over, turned around, and faced my enemies (who were tripping me in their minds) and the man who was taking this ridiculous scenario very seriously. I asked him if it was okay to go, and he said anytime. So I said, "Hello, ladies and gentlemen. Welcome to the Laugh Factory. We have a great show for you tonight. Our first comic has performed at clubs all over the country. You might have seen him on *The Late Show with David Letterman* or *The Tonight Show*. I know you're gonna like him, so please give a warm welcome to Mike Roberts." Then I just looked at the other comics. It was then I noticed that someone from the club had come up to the guy running the audition and asked him a question, and he was winding up his answer. I don't know if he heard any of my intro, which was a shame because I *killed!* I said the fictional comedian's name just right, smiled, even led the audience applause. All for naught.

I am sure when he heard no more noise coming out of my mouth he thought that must be it. He looked up at me and said, "Great. We'll let ya know. Do you remember how to get back downstairs?" I told him I did, then thanked him and took the windy staircase down. After finding my way through the club construction, I stepped back out onto Sunset Boulevard. As I got into my car, I had a moment of "What the hell just happened?" I didn't know what to do with that, so I just started the car and drove home.

And other times, I had bad auditions.

DARKER DAYS

I was taking just about any job at this point. It didn't really matter how little I made, except in regard to making rent. I was living the dream—as long as I was in the right frame of mind.

When I was in the *wrong* frame of mind, *that* was when it got pretty dark. When Steve and I first got our own place in L.A., we didn't know the neighborhoods, and we ended up renting an apartment in an area that we later read in the paper was home to four gangs vying for control of the neighborhood. In the time we lived there, we had our cars broken into and arrived home to see cops with their doors winged and guns drawn. On one occasion, I was walking up the outside steps leading to our front door when a guy in the passenger seat of a really nice car parked at the curb yelled to me, "Hey! Knock on that door and see if anyone answers it." It was the door of the apartment right under us. I knocked on it, and then the guy said, "Good. Now go up to your apartment and shut your door." I did as I was told.

We moved shortly thereafter.

I had just one credit card, which my dad had given me for gas for the trip. It was a Mobil gas card. (That was the extent of financial aid from my pop, but it helped *a lot*. He wasn't overly crazy about me moving to L.A.) For the first month, everything we ate came from a Mobil mini-mart and didn't need refrigeration. (Apartments didn't come with refrigerators then.) We ate a lot of Doritos that first month. I remember getting a call from my dad asking how I had spent $400 at Mobil since arriving. He thought I had bought tires.

There were days early on when I had no gas in my car, less than $20 in my bank account, and could afford for meals only the ninety-nine-cent Coney dogs at the 7-11. It is kind of fun writing about it now, but at the moment I remember thinking, "This is *not* going as planned."

Religion was nonexistent for me at this point in my life. Despite that, I felt like I had to keep at this because it was what I truly believed God *wanted* me to do. This was what I was created for. These gifts I had were *meant* to be used in this way. What I couldn't figure out was why it was so hard. Was I going through this ordeal so that I could write about my "struggling years" later, after I started hosting *The Tonight Show*? (I got it half right, I guess.) I don't ever remember questioning if comedy was what God wanted me to do. I don't even remember questioning if God wanted me famous. Of course God did. But if that was the case, why wasn't the dream coming true?

After Laura moved out to L.A. to be near me, we visited churches but could not find a fit. Honestly, I didn't try that hard. The only reason we looked at all was because it was the norm for us, having grown up in churchgoing families. Laura had been Methodist all her life, and that's the reason we looked into Methodist churches. It didn't really matter to me. (If Laura had been raised in a Lutheran church, I might be a Lutheran pastor now. Thank God she wasn't raised Catholic, or I would be a priest and we would have been dating in secret all these years.)

I remember walking into Burbank United Methodist Church and seeing old people and their parents—thirteen of them. Not for me. That might have been the last church I walked into for about ten years. I didn't have anything against the church. It just felt useless. When I see new people in their twenties walk into my church now, I often think back to how I felt about church in my twenties. Are we relevant to them? Are we useless to them? Maybe.

HUSTLIN'

There are two kinds of lousy jobs: the ones within the entertainment industry and the "normal jobs." I expected normal jobs to suck. They were the jobs I just took to get by. Most of mine were minimum wage jobs. I hated them but actually not too much because I went in *knowing* they sucked. There were no surprises.

It's true that most people will do almost anything to make it in Hollywood. I took a job in the first few months of being there that embarrassed me and makes me feel dirty. To this day, I still feel like there was a momentary lapse in my moral compass. I want to forget about it, but I needed the money, and while I wouldn't do it again, I did what I had to do at the time.

I was a telemarketer.

I saw an ad that said I had the potential to make more than five hundred dollars a week. That was huge money to me. I answered the ad and was told to come on down. (Always be leery when the ad says you have "the potential" to make a lot of money. You also have "the potential" to win the lottery.)

I showed up at a small, nondescript building across from the NBC studios in Burbank. This area is populated with tons of small, depressing buildings in most of which workers handled postproduction tasks for the studios and networks. It almost felt like I was in show business.

I soon discovered that I was working for a telemarketing company that had the testosterone of Wall Street but without the money. It was a nightmare.

We sold copier toner over the phone. When we arrived in the morning, we were told to grab a copy of the Yellow Pages. We then took a dozen index cards and stuck them at random places throughout the book. Then we'd open the book to each card and find the most promising-looking business on the page.

These were our leads.

Our job was to call the business on the page and ask to talk to the purchasing manager. If the person on the other line said "Hang on," we would hang up. What we wanted to hear was that the purchasing manager was at lunch or on vacation and could this person help us?

We would then say that we had a toner order for the company but wanted to verify the copier make and model so we were sure to send the right product. The person would read off the copier make and model, and we would place an order for the toner that matched the copier. This kept us within the law; these companies were getting a

product that worked—it was just marked up a billion percent. Once we "verified" the order (which had never been
placed by the purchasing manager, but we had now been
given verbal confirmation over the phone), we were home
free. We would verify the address by reading it out of the
phonebook, and we would "get that order out to them
right away."

We all sat at little, cramped gunmetal gray desks with
our phonebooks and would dial for dollars all day long. If
anyone gave us too much pushback, we could either hang
up or pound on the side of our desk to notify the boss sitting
at the front of the room that we needed help. Really classy.
He would pick up the extensions, because we were "turning over the order to our supervisor, who would provide
them with better customer service and answer any questions they might have." He would bully them into the order
or hang up, though I rarely remember that happening. If we
locked down the sale, it was a 10 percent commission, and
it would go up from there at different thresholds. It was just
this side of the law—by a hair.

I lasted two days.

I realized that while I had a gift for gab, I couldn't use
it this way. It really did feel dirty. Regardless of whether
or not it passed the letter of the law, it felt morally wrong.
I realized then that I had a moral limit. Some people could
do this and sleep like a baby at night. I was not one of those
people. Granted, the companies got a product that they
paid for (and dearly), but it was a con, pure and simple.
I have always loved those movies where there was a con
and a mark (*Paper Moon, The Sting, The Hustler, Ocean's
Eleven*), but I discovered that it is one thing to watch the
movie and something very different to pull the con. I don't
have the stomach for it.

As bad as the "normal" jobs were, though (if you can call a barely legal con job "normal"), the crappy entertainment jobs were more insidious. They varied in a lot of ways, but what they all had in common was a certain level of humiliation. Technically, they were showbiz jobs. But deep down, I knew they were embarrassing jobs. True, there is no such thing as small parts, only small people, but it is safe to say there are no superstars fighting for these jobs.

I worked at CNN. I was "interning." This meant I worked for free. I couldn't get the internship without lying and saying I was still in school. I faked a letter from Cal State Northridge that recommended me. It was never even opened, just put in my file. For the effort of being sneaky, I got to get everyone lunch and get stars sodas. Few jobs taught me more about hard work paying off and taught me, *really* taught me, about humility.

I emceed corporate picnics. I hosted all kinds of lawn games for law firms in Malibu, but because of the strict sound ordinances there, we weren't allowed to use any amplification. That meant I had to shout directions and "host" three hundred to five hundred people without a mic. I would do two picnics a weekend and have absolutely no voice on Monday morning, week after week. None. This was one of the toughest situations I have ever performed in, but I loved it. It taught me how to command a crowd (rarely have I had a tougher group than three hundred L.A. lawyers and their families.)

One of the jobs I thought would be great initially but that turned into a nightmare was an advertising campaign for Pepsi with Ray Charles singing, "You got the right one, baby." What sounded cool (being part of a nationwide campaign) turned into me standing next to Pepsi displays with a karaoke machine in the aisle of a Sam's Club. I prayed,

literally prayed, that I wouldn't see anyone I knew. I think
I got lucky with that gig. That job taught me to always read
the fine print and know that nothing is as good as it might
seem at first glance.

I was an assistant at a talent agency for a while. There
was the owner/agent, a guy who booked literary talent, a
guy who booked clubs, and a guy who booked cruise ships.
I had a lot of "other duties as assigned." One of those was
to put a videotape, a headshot, and a note in a collection of
packets: "Per our discussion, here is the information you
requested about so-and-so. Feel free to reach out to me if
you have any questions. Sincerely, [name]." Then I handed
each note to the agent, had him sign it, and put the packet in
the mail. One time I was asked to erase audition videotapes
of comics who had sucked. (Hey, free blank tapes for our
comics to use!) As I was doing that, the head agent came
in, did a double take, and asked me who had told me to do
that. I said the other agent had. At the sound of his name
being shouted, the junior agent came out of his office. The
senior agent proceeded to shout, "Did you tell Jerry to do
that?" When the junior agent tried to answer, the senior
agent just said, "Shut up! Shut the f#$% up! You are never
to talk to him again. Who the f#$% told you to talk to him?
When did he become your f#$%ing assistant? Don't say a
f#$%ing word." Then pointing to the guy, the senior agent
said to me, "See this guy? He is no one. He is a f#$%ing
idiot. Never listen to another f#$%ing word he says, you
got that?" I just kind of nodded. It was like a tornado just
touched down at my desk in the hallway, blew everything
up, and then went on its way.

I grew up in the Midwest; we just didn't talk like that
in our house. (Sadly, I was a quick learner and now do have
a potty mouth, but not that bad!) After the senior agent had

left, I walked into the junior agent's office and said I was so sorry that happened. He looked at me like I had two heads. He said, "For what?" I said for the way the senior agent went off on him. He said, "That? Don't worry about that. That's just the way he is." L.A. sure was a lot different from Michigan.

I had a bit part in a movie once. My roommate Steve knew a woman named Susanna who was the assistant casting director at the Casting Company, which was, fittingly, *the* casting company in Hollywood. They did all the big movies. Susanna helped get me in to see one of the owners, and before I knew it, I was offered two days of work on the John Hughes film *Dutch,* starring Ed O'Neill. I was to play what was originally a soldier coming home on a bus for the holidays. That got changed when the studio realized our real soldiers weren't coming home from Desert Storm for the holidays, so my part became a punk on a bus with two other punks who stole the child lead's shoes.

I am sure you remember the part. Susanna fought hard to get my character a name, but in the end she lost that battle. When the credits rolled, I played the pivotal role "White Man on Bus." If there was to be a sequel, I was hoping for "White Man on Plane" or "White Man on Boat." Unfortunately, said sequel was never made. When the movie came out, I was in about five to seven minutes of it. It was more than half a dozen pages of dialogue and a pretty decent scene. Some of it got cut when it went to HBO. A little more of the scene was cut when it went to free cable, and still more when it went to network. Every so often it is on the air still, and the scene is a blink! Having said that, I still get residual checks from Twentieth Century

Fox; my last one was for eighty-three cents. I think they lost money mailing it to me.

Then there was the time I got to do the audience warm-up for *America's Funniest People*. I was so fired up; I was pretty hyper. So hyper, in fact, that when I ran out from the wings, my fancy leather-bottom dress shoes caught the top step of the stage set, and my feet went flying out from under me. I landed on my ass so hard that I bent the metal business-card case in my pocket. There was a collective gasp until I leaped up. It got a huge laugh—but not the kind I wanted.

And between all these gigs, I was saying over the bar in my entertainment-strained voice, "What can I get ya?"

THE HAPPIEST PLACE ON EARTH

The year 1989 was both the best of times and the worst of times for me. It was the best of times because I was working. I was running in a hundred directions at once and making connections all over Hollywood. It was the worst of times because I was starving. Most of my jobs paid just above minimum wage, and the weekend emceeing gigs paid a hundred dollars. It wasn't *awful* money, but this was L.A., one of the most expensive cities in the world to live in. I just wasn't making ends meet.

There was an open audition for a job as a host at Disneyland, and I figured, why not? What have I got to lose? Auditioning was something I could do in my sleep at this point, and I needed to find a more solid gig. I auditioned in a room with about two hundred other guys who were six feet tall, weighed 185 pounds, and had brown hair and brown eyes. Odds were slim.

The audition was on a Tuesday, and we were told that we would know by the end of the business day on Friday. It was one of the longest weeks of my life.

When Friday came, there had been no call. I am normally pretty calm when I don't get the job after an audition (which was a lot), but I really wanted this one, and I knew I could do it. Five o'clock came . . . and went. To say I was devastated would be, well, actually, an overstatement. I wasn't *devastated,* but I was pretty wrecked. I needed a break. I was burnt out, I was killing myself with effort and had nothing to show for it. At 5:10 p.m., I told Steve that I was going for a drive. I couldn't stand how pathetic I felt staring at the phone.

I didn't know where I would go; I didn't want to waste gas, but I was in pretty bad shape. The garage in our apartment complex was underneath the building, so I started descending the stairs. Just then, I heard our apartment door swing open and Steve scream down to me, "Jerry, don't go! It's them! On the phone!" I ran back upstairs, touching barely three steps, and got on the phone. "Hey Jerry, sorry the call is late. We are crazy busy. We would like to make you a formal offer of full-time employment as one of our Dream Machine hosts celebrating Disneyland's 35th anniversary. It will be $32,500 a year with full benefits and will last exactly one year from January 1 through December 31. Would you like the job?" I told him I would, and he gave me the details on where to show up and when. I thanked him and hung up the phone.

I headed back downstairs to go for that drive with a very different feeling. Before I got in the car, I fell to my knees. It was the first time I had ever done that. I was so thankful. I knelt there and cried. It was as if in an instant I had won the lottery. $32,500? I had never made that kind of money in my life, *and* it was a steady entertainment job? For a *year? Plus* dental? Comics never get dental! I couldn't believe it.

I don't think I had acknowledged to myself how much I was struggling just to survive in L.A. It was a hard place to live in, especially when you're there with the goal of making all your dreams come true. But all that is easy to forget when you're working in the happiest place on earth and making other people's dreams come true.

People visiting Disneyland during that thirty-fifth anniversary year came up to "the Dream Machine" with a lucky ticket they had received at the front gate. We asked them a few inane questions and had them pull a giant slot-machinelike handle. Every day we gave away two round-trip tickets anywhere in the continental United States, two $500 savings bonds, and tons and tons of videos, watches, and stuffed animals. We also gave away a car. Every day. At some point in the day, you would hear the dry ice kick in, and the top of the cake in front of us would lift up. A car would rise up through the smoke and out of the center of the giant thirty-fifth anniversary cake like a mechanical stripper at a guy's bachelor party. Other hosts worked with me, but I myself gave thirty-seven cars away that year. It was fun year. I felt like a really, really rich Santa Claus.

Disneyland was a trip. You walked around "backstage" and you saw Tinkerbell talking about getting wasted the night before, which freaked me out at first. I mean, it's not like I really *thought* she had wings, but I didn't think she was a college student who could shotgun beers.

Working at Disneyland kicked off a number of things. Two of the other full-time hosts also worked as warm-up comics for television shows and were able to toss me some gigs. After the year was up, I was booked to do a number of special events for Disney's marketing and entertainment divisions. These were just odd, one-time gigs, but I would take them. I never knew which gig was going to be *the* gig, and I was always hoping the *next one* was going to be the one that took me to the next level.

CHAPTER 3

CAREFUL WHAT YOU WISH FOR

Eventually I started getting gigs more in line with what I dreamed I'd do: professional comedy. All the time I was still bartending and slowly piecing a career together.

I took a comedy writing class at UCLA that was being taught by Bob Basso, the original Bozo the Clown. It was a great class, and it taught me the difference between being funny and being a comedian. A lot of people can be funny after a few beers or at the company sales kickoff. As my brother said to me once, "You want to know if you are a comedian? Can you be funny right after you got in a fight with your girlfriend? Can you be funny when you just got in a car wreck? Can you be funny with a 102-degree fever? *Then* you are a comedian." That UCLA class led to auditioning for a master class being taught by Budd Friedman, the owner of the Improv. He was considered the godfather of comedy. I got in. I learned not only how to construct a set but, without knowing it at the time, how to write a sermon—flow, structure, pacing, tone, inflection. Every preacher should take a class in stand-up writing and performance.

The best part of that class was it gave me what I needed: essentially a 10-week audition to work at the Improv. Seven weeks into the class, I got a job as the doorman at the Improv in Hollywood.

It was about to get very real, very quick.

Budd was a horrific boss. Worst I ever had. One time he said to me in front of a couple dozen people while I was working the front door, "Put one foot on the black tile, one on the white tile. Can you handle that? Is that too hard? Are you an idiot?" Awful stuff, but he had every comic in L.A. where he wanted them because his was the club that could open doors, and I put up with the treatment because he was the godfather of comedy and he gave me a chance. He moved me from the front-door guy to the emcee in the showroom to the house emcee within a couple of months. Once in the room, I got to watch the greatest comics of the time work out material: Jay Leno, Paul Reiser, Dennis Miller, Bill Maher, Drew Carey, Adam Sandler, David Spade, Sam Kinison, and many more. I watched them work, learned their tricks, and talked to them about the craft between sets. It was like working at Birdland in the 1950s. They all treated me as one of the guys, though we all knew I wasn't. They were made men. I was still the errand boy. I didn't care. The very fact they let me sit there and listen in on their conversations was nothing less than magic for me.

Just getting to work at the Improv was a pretty big deal. It was ground zero of the comedy boom of the late 1980s and early '90s. Working there was like saying you went to Juilliard or Harvard. Once you got accepted *there*, your road was a bit easier. In some ways, if you had Budd's blessing, you also had access to people you never in a million years would have had access to otherwise.

I had just started working there and was seating people in the restaurant. I was standing at the host stand talking to Jerry Seinfeld. He was already huge in the world of stand-up, but his television show *Seinfeld* hadn't started yet. I think I was so blown away to have alone time with him that I started asking more and more questions about comedy rather than just having a conversation. At one point, he looked at me and said, "Are we just two guys talking, or are you asking me for advice?" I was totally busted. I figured, well, if this is the last time we ever talk and from this point on there will be a restraining order on me, I might as well get something out of it. I said to him, "Well, maybe we are just two guys talking . . . and one is asking for advice." He looked at me and said seriously (comics are *a lot* more serious about their craft than most people believe), "I would suggest that you get on stage two times a night, every night for three years, then you can cut back to once a night." I thanked him and thought about that a lot. There is something to be learned from a work ethic no matter what the profession. Discipline matters. I took that lesson with me throughout the years. If all the crap I had to put up with from Budd Friedman was the cost of having that moment, it was worth it.

THE IMPROV AUDITION

It was the most important 240 seconds of my life. It would literally determine the future course of my career. Everything hinged on these four minutes. No pressure.

It's an odd feeling. That feeling you get when you feel as if your whole life's work is resting on this one moment. The sense that everything you have worked for up to this moment is on the line in the next four minutes. I have had similar moments a number of times, but none with the pressure of an all-or-nothing scenario like this one. Every comic in L.A. in the late 1980s had a similar experience. For some, it would be the beginning of a launch into stardom, the gateway into the big time. For others, it would haunt them for years.

I had up to this point negotiated the rushing waters of stand-up in L.A. pretty well. I knew if I got into the UCLA class, I could probably get passed to the master class, which with Budd as its teacher, would probably get me a better chance to land a job at his club. All was going as planned as I moved quickly from doorman to emcee, but the audition was a different thing. Having "a slot" at the club was another big step up. It meant that Budd and Mark Lanow (Budd's partner) saw star potential in you.

The audition process was simple: Do four minutes of your set and get off the stage. After that, you would get notes from Mark and told whether you "passed" or not.

To get on the stage in the first place was something of an ordeal in itself. More than a hundred comics would show up on the specified day each month. Each would draw a number, and those who drew numbers one through fifteen got an audition slot—three months later. So your chances for the open audition were fifteen out of a hundred or more. You could go months and not be one of the fifteen. Tough break.

If you're lucky enough to get the audition, you then spend the next three months honing the tightest four minutes of your life. Four minutes is not a lot of time to show what you've got, especially to Mark, who has seen thousands of comics. You find any stage that will take you, and you get up there with your mini cassette recorder and do your set, making adjustments in timing, word choice (is "ointment" funnier than "balm"?), and inflection—over and over and over and over.

Then you tell everybody. I mean *everybody:* friends, colleagues, friends of colleagues, colleagues of friends, strangers on the street, the guy who works the drive-through. You flip over every stone. With any luck, half will show. I had worked a long time telling jokes, and I wanted people to see that the hard work paid off. I wanted to show people that I wasn't just *saying* I was a comedian. I *was* one. (Plus, it helps to have a packed house—and it doesn't hurt the Improv that all those people are coming. It's a business, after all.)

I had been performing for a number of years at this point. I had thousands of performances behind me. I felt like I had a pretty tight four minutes, something to be proud of. As a result, I invited everyone: current girlfriend, old girlfriends, roommates, coworkers, industry professionals, bartenders, servers. Pretty much everyone I knew within a fifty-mile radius. And they all came. It was a packed house.

It's an exciting feeling knowing that you do something well and getting to share it with people. I don't have that feeling about a lot of things. I suck at sports, was only average at karate, and just a solid B student at school. To be *good* at something is a pretty great feeling.

One by one, we were introduced and we took the stage, bam bam bam. It was like churning out meat—one after the other. Then my name was called and I bounced up on stage.

I bombed.

When you are bombing, you know within seconds. Something is off. You often can't name it. But you are certain. I got laughs in all the right places, just not long enough. I kept my cool, but I could feel the flop sweat running down my back. Still, I stayed calm and felt like it was solid. But deep down, I knew it wasn't my best. (My friends later confirmed that by offering me comments like "You looked good up there" and "Really well done." Everything but "funny.") Not only did I bomb. I bombed in front of everyone I knew in L.A.

After the performance, you go over and stand in line to talk to Mark as if you are waiting in line at an ATM. One by one, you get your turn to have him "give you notes."

My turn came up, and Mark read off his notes. "Jerry, really professional up there. You looked like you had done it a thousand times—which is part of the problem. You look slick, like a vaudeville comic. You just need to find your voice. It's not that you don't look good up there. You're just not funny. We're gonna pass."

Those words stopped me in my tracks. Not the "we're gonna pass"—that was a crap shoot. But "you're just not funny"? Coming from a guy who sees and judges funny people for a living? If anyone would know funny, it's Mark. If he said it, it must be true. The *one thing* I thought I knew for *sure,* I was wrong about. What else was I wrong about?

I now realize he was right—on both counts. Still, those words haunted me for more than a decade.

That night was a turning point. Something died in me that night. It would be a while before something new would get reborn.

STAND-UP ON THE ROAD

In my mind, what would mark me as a professional, rather than someone who just had a hobby, was to be a working comic on the road.

I got my wish—and hated it.

It was rarely what you see on television. Even the shitty parts look okay on TV. It was more pathetic when you lived it. Part of the reason was the moment in time.

The late 1980s and early '90s was a time when comedy was exploding. In 1980, there were only 10 full-time paying comedy clubs in the country. By the mid '80s, clubs started popping up all over the place. There was some sort of "Chuckles Comedy Emporium" or a "Yuck Yucks" in every city in the nation. For the top comics, this was a huge windfall. It meant more (and better) places to make money. For those just starting out, however, not so much.

Many noncomedy clubs that were looking for any way to bring in a crowd started doing "comedy nights." These were places that had no interest in the art form of comedy, and you sure as hell weren't going to get famous playing them. Not even clubs, they were basically just your neighborhood bar and grill, trying the latest thing to make a buck.

The money was unbelievable, but not in a good way. On average, I would drive about five hours for sixty dollars and two drink tickets. I would get a room in some place like a Motel 6 and do one show on Thursday night and two shows on both Friday and Saturday. I felt like the man who would go behind the elephant in the parade with a shovel and scoop anything the elephant left behind on the parade route. He was telling a guy at the bar what he did, and the guy said, "That's awful. Why don't you quit?" The man answered, "What? And give up showbiz?"

One time I was doing a gig at a bar and grill in the middle of nowhere. I was ready to go on, but there was no stage. The bartender told me that guys do the show from the end of the bar in the waitresses' service well because that's as far as the mic reached. He also asked me for a favor. With a straight face, fresh stitches, and most of his teeth, he said to me, "Listen, the regulars here really like *The Simpsons*. Are you cool if we put off the show by a half hour so the guys can watch it?" Of course I said yes, and so I sat at the bar watching cartoons that were funnier than me essentially open for me. After that was over, he put up the screen and handed me the mic. The only thing that made the gig worse was that the mic cord wasn't quite long enough, so I did my whole set hunched over. I looked like the hunchback of open mic.

What? And give up showbiz?

MALL SANTA

I had worked a lot of lousy jobs, but at least they were creative. (My longtime barber in L.A. once said to me, "Every time you come in here you either have the shittiest job I have ever heard of or the coolest.") When I took a job at the Gap, I knew it wasn't cool *and* it wasn't shitty. It was just . . . normal. That made it even worse.

Working at the Gap during Christmas is a special slice of hell everyone should try at least once. Months earlier at the Burbank mall, I saw a sign advertising for mall Santas, and I thought I could use the cash. It was eye opening to see who actually applied, and more surprising to see who got hired to be Santas that Christmas. I remember a disproportionate number of bikers. Few if any of them needed to take the time to "apply" a beard—or even take the time to bathe daily.

There were very few rules regarding being a Santa: don't curse at the children, don't hit any parents (but apparently hitting *on* a parent was not a hard-and-fast rule; I heard a number of my fellow Santas say some things that just felt wrong coming out of a jolly old elf's mouth), don't show up to your shift drunk. It seemed to me that "Don't show up to work drunk" was one of those rules you don't have to state. It should be a given.

I was wrong.

I think we lost nearly half a dozen Santas because they had hit the bottle prior to coming to sit on Santa's throne. It was a lot more than eggnog on their breath too. Poor bastards. I hope they found other gigs.

I was pretty good at being Santa, although it was pretty clear I was wearing a fake beard and had a pillow under my jacket. I think the parents were pleased with my "Santaness." I laughed deeply, never promised anything to the kids, and avoided hitting on the moms. While that may look like the bare minimum a Santa should strive for, it propelled me to the top of the St. Nick food chain. I got great shifts that worked around my Gap schedule, although sometimes the gigs would be back to back, which meant that I occasionally went into the Gap with my eyebrows still painted white. That's an odd look when you are trying to make it work with relaxed-fit chinos and a salt-colored polo. (None of the Gap's colors are actual colors. They are "salt" and "cloud" and "snow.")

While I was good at being a Santa, and clearly "gifted," it wasn't all tinsel and sugar cookies. I often got peed on. More often than you would think. In fact, it is the dominant memory I have of being a mall Santa. Kids just get so excited by the fact that they are actually *seeing* Santa and sitting on his lap that bladder control becomes secondary.

I also got thrown up on more than once, and that was a bigger deal, as it facilitated Santa having to "go feed the reindeer out back." I changed into a different Santa outfit that no doubt had also been peed on and thrown up on but that had had a trip to the dry cleaner since.

The Santa gig wasn't awful. It just wasn't what I wanted to be doing. I was thirty and wasn't on the street or completely broke. I just wasn't *fulfilled.* This was also a bit of a problem. As a result of this, I now found myself feeling guilty for feeling bad when I knew so many others had it so much worse.

I started to think while I was at the Gap and being Santa that while I loved being in front of a crowd, I didn't like memorizing lines like an actor and for a comedian I wasn't that, well, funny. I was polished and slick but just not all that funny. Unfortunately, funny is one of the minimum requirements for a comedian. I was a very good emcee and host. I knew how to engage an audience and keep the energy up. I could even motivate them to do crazy shit. Once they discovered I wasn't going to make fun of them— once they realized that no one was going to look more the fool than me—they would go with me anywhere.

It was around this time I realized that in addition to comics, I also loved anyone who could stand in front of people and motivate them: Wayne Dyer, Marianne Williamson, Deepak Chopra, Bernie Siegel. They were people who engaged their audiences alone, the only character they played was themselves, and they motivated people to do better.

I wanted to be a motivational speaker. Of course, I didn't realize that at the time. But that was what intrigued me. I didn't mind making people laugh, and I did it all the time on stage. It just didn't feel like enough. I wanted people to do more than just laugh. I wanted them to think. I wanted them to be a better version of themselves. I wanted people to be the *best* version of themselves.

I had one problem. No one is going to take motivational advice from a thirty-year-old jean-folding, Santa-suit wearing, semi-funny stand-up comic.

I tried to start thinking about other jobs where I could stand in front of people, motivate them to be their best selves, offer them hope, and be myself.

That last part proved to be the hardest. I didn't know how to be "nothing but myself," as cummings said. I still couldn't envision being anything other than a stand-up comic or game show host or talk show host. I liked the idea of motivating people and giving people hope, but I knew I didn't have the credentials of Wayne Dyer or the teeth of Anthony Robbins. People who were like me didn't inspire people. They just made them laugh and got paid. I didn't think I had any other abilities. And I was starting to wonder if I even had those.

Even if at this point I would have *allowed* myself to be a minister, I knew the powers that be would kick me out: I didn't talk, act, behave like any minister I had ever heard of. I knew I had an ego and wanted to be liked, and clergy didn't have those issues, right? (Obviously, I didn't know many clergy.) It's too easy to let others decide your worth or define what you can do or be. It can be hard to see your gifts in a different light. You might think that your gift is in the doing when your gift is really in the teaching. To this day, I think I am better as a "comedy doctor," punching up an existing routine, than I ever was as an actual comic. I am still a better presentation-skills coach than I am a public speaker. I knew I was off; I just didn't know all my options.

I knew pretty early on that being a traditional stand-up comic was not going to be my route, but it was the closest thing to what I thought was "my thing" that I knew of. What I liked to do was throw a party and be a host. I was always a better emcee than a comedian. I knew how to keep a room alive, and when it was down I could bring it back up. I also knew when a comic was killing it. I knew to shut up and let it ride and when to get on to the next comic.

I was never the main attraction. People always came to see whoever it was I was introducing. I was the one who told them about the headliner and got them excited about the headliner, but it was always about making people focus on the main attraction. Bring the spotlight to the headliner—*that* is what the gig was about. It was never supposed to be about me. It was about who was coming up next.

Chapter 4
BROKEN WINDOWS, BROKEN DREAMS

Glass was flying everywhere. I ducked down behind the bar and prayed it would stop. People were screaming and running, and the owner was grabbing his gun. It was apparent at that moment that I was not getting paid enough.

The South Central riots in 1992 marked the worst loss of life during a riot since the New York City draft riots in 1863—yep, eighteen sixty-three!

Los Angeles had a lot of racial tension going into the Rodney King trial, which included video of the police beating Rodney King after he had been pulled over. The officers were acquitted of any wrongdoing, even though it appeared clear on the tape that there was excessive force. This trial verdict set off six days of rioting during which fifty-three people were killed and over two thousand people injured.

In the beginning, the rioting was isolated in the south central part of Los Angeles, but over the next few days, it spread all over the city.

I had just landed a bartending job a few months prior at an upscale pool hall in Pasadena called Q's. With three stories, it had an amazing triangle bar at street level and then additional bars upstairs and downstairs. It was a huge, huge place.

Truth be told, I was in way over my head. We were slammed every night three deep at the bar the whole night long. I was ringing over twelve hundred dollars in cheap beer during a 10:30-to-1:30 shift even at the little upstairs bar, not including the servers I was pouring for. I did not have that level of skill, and it damn near killed me. The money was great, but I was always toast after those shifts.

We rotated bars, and one night I was working the main bar in the front of the club. It was always fun to work there at that gorgeous mahogany triangle bar, but it was crazy busy. The club was located on a main drag in Pasadena, next to railroad tracks that cut right between buildings. Every time a train went by, we would run "train shot" specials for a buck for the duration of the train's passing. These were watered-down, premade shots that cost nothing to make but sold like crazy when a train went by. We couldn't collect the money fast enough.

This night was in early May, and although we had heard about the verdict and the riot, that was way down in South Central, nowhere near us. We were safe.

Or so we thought.

About halfway through the night we were greeted with a train roaring by. This sent a mad dash to the bar. What we weren't aware of was that in the middle of the street, maybe a hundred feet from the front door but on the other side of the train, a large group was forming with rocks and sticks and bricks, and they were pissed.

As soon as the train went by, we breathed a sigh of relief that was quickly replaced by the sound of breaking glass. A group of people stood in front of the floor-to-ceiling windows that were at the front of the club and heaved rocks and bricks at the glass, sending broken glass flying everywhere. People were screaming, and it was bedlam. While the owner went to get his gun, patrons went running for cover and, like all good bartenders that you watched in westerns, we ducked behind the bar as low as we could.

We heard the owner screaming, telling servers and anyone else to go and try to get to their cars. We locked down the drawers and got ready to make the dash. The crowd outside moved down the street to do damage to the Bath and Body Works, the Banana Republic, the AMC movie theater, and the Gap.

About three-quarters of the way to my car, I heard someone scream, "They're coming back!" Sure enough, the crowd had decided to turn around. I have no idea if they were doing harm to human beings, but I thought it best not to take time to find out. With weatherman hair and pasty white skin, I looked like your average suburban middle-aged, able-bodied white guy—the kind of guy who generally does not fare well in altercations during civil unrest.

I remember getting to my car and trying to start it, and having visions of it not starting as I continued to try, watching the angry mob get closer like they do in those zombie films. I did not want my brains eaten. I didn't even want a bruise. Because this wasn't a horror movie but real life, the car started on the first try, and I sped back to Burbank.

I went to Dalt's, the restaurant adjacent to the Warner Brothers lot where Laura, now my fiancée, was working. When I walked in, still breathing hard from the adrenaline, it was like walking into another world: Everyone was eating and drinking and doing their thing. There was laughter and the normal business of a weekend night. A few people were watching the riots on the TVs in the bar, but for the most part, it was business as usual.

Laura was startled to see me and asked why I wasn't at Q's. I told her, but it all sounded like a fairytale given my current surroundings. It really was like a totally different world.

I realized that night that while we all live in the same world, we really don't. For so many people living their lives on the margins or living with unimaginable frustration with the unfairness of systemic racism, the world is a very different place. In some ways, for them, every day is a horror movie, and they don't get to get away from their troubles nearly as easily as I did. As Martin Luther King Jr. said, "A riot is the language of the unheard." There was a deeper frustration taking place than I would ever experience. (Recent riots in Ferguson, Mo., Baltimore, and other places remind me how little has changed in twenty years.)

ALL SHOOK UP

The morning of January 17, 1994, sucked—specifically 4:31 a.m. Normally I don't remember much at 4:31 in the morning. Either it has been an unusually heavy drinking night and well, let's face it, by then I'm not remembering much, or (preferably) the lights are out and I'm tucked away in bed.

That morning was neither. At 4:30, I was fast asleep, but one minute later a 6.7 magnitude earthquake rocked Los Angeles, and for the first time in my thirty years, I thought I was going to die.

I was working at one of the least enthralling of the 1,678 jobs I had had in my life up to that point. This particular job was managing a store called *Successories*, which specialized in motivational tapes, posters that said things like, "There's no 'I' in TEAM," and crystal eagles that were usually given to top salespeople at pharmaceutical companies. The store was in a mall in Southern California and was about the size of four changing rooms in a standard Gap. No one came in. Ever. You can only adjust tapes and posters and dust them so much. Some days we would have sales of $8.31—for the whole day. Someone would come in and buy a few crappy "You can't soar like an eagle and hang out with turkeys" postcards, and that would be the sales for the day. This was the job (we have all had them) where, at the beginning of the day, I would pull a yellow legal pad out of the drawer and write "480" at the top. Half an hour later, I would write "450." I would continue this throughout the day, writing just how many minutes I had left until I could grab that giant metal hook and pull down the gate across the front of the store, count the $8.31 we had made, and then go home and mentally prepare to do it all again the next day.

Little did I know that when I closed up shop on January 16, it would be the last time that store would be standing.

Northridge, California, was the epicenter of the earthquake in 1994, which would be forever known as the Northridge earthquake. The Northridge mall, which was in the center of Northridge, was destroyed. Had the earthquake hit six hours later, anyone working in that store would have been killed.

Fortunately, that was not the case, and I was sound asleep—until the earthquake hit.

You always see earthquakes as these rumbling, shaking things. That was not my experience. It felt like someone had lifted the end of our bed four feet high and dropped it. Hard.

Laura and I immediately leapt out of bed and grabbed our earthquake kits (everyone had them) and ran to the door frame in the bedroom. I remember thinking that I didn't want to die like this: mostly naked with an earthquake kit in my hand. I also remember thinking, "You should probably check to make sure Laura is okay." (Chivalry apparently *was* dead—at least for me in that moment.).

After the initial quake, there were a couple more big ones, then *thousands* of little ones over the next few days. We slept in our car the next night. (You do not want to be on the third floor of an apartment building if it shook again.) After we got out of the building, we headed down to the pool, which was at the center of the complex. It was surreal, all these people walking around in their pajamas, with radios and flashlights in the near dark. It looked like something out of *Close Encounters of the Third Kind*. We sat around on pool deck chairs, trying to tune in our radios and hear exactly how much of our city was destroyed.

As it turned out, a lot. Complete freeways collapsed. Entire blocks of homes and apartments were destroyed. More than 5,000 people were injured, and more than twenty billion dollars of property was destroyed. Not to mention the mind screw the earthquake did on people. It is safe to say this was the straw that broke our camel's back.

We left L.A. within three months.

We weren't the only ones. Scores of people said, "Screw it," and hit the road. Some packed up their stuff and left *that night*. We didn't leave right away, but we knew we were at the end of our ropes.

The earthquake also had an interesting effect on people in the coming weeks. The week after the earthquake, the restaurant Laura worked at ran out of steaks and vodka. Apparently, the three-martini lunch was back in fashion, and a rib eye at midday was not that big a deal any more. In addition, the restaurant sold more desserts than ever

before. Who cares about love handles when you are under
two tons of rubble?

Near-death experiences are markers. They remind
us that we don't have forever. They remind us to stop fucking around and start really working for what we want. They
remind us of what's important, joyful, and meaningful in
our lives.

WHAT REALLY MATTERS?

It's actually pretty easy to talk about "focusing on what
really matters" or "living in the moment." At one time, I
could have sold you some postcards and posters saying
those very things. The talking about it is easy. It's cheap.
Living it is hard. I wasted so many years chasing things that
matter so little. There are so many clichés around this that
it feels lame to even talk about it. Yet so often we don't get
the message. We get one pass at this life. One. Not to get all
Eminem on everybody, but if you had one shot, one opportunity to seize everything you every wanted—okay, you get
the idea. We know this! But we bail. We don't want to get
burned again. We don't want to get disappointed again. We
don't want to get hurt again. Pain is a bitch. It keeps us from
giving things a shot. It keeps us from reaching. It keeps us
from even *trying* again. So we bounce. We move on to the
next thing—the safe thing. The irony is, choosing the safe
thing is dangerous in the long run.

I can look back in my journal and see where I was
gripping the pen in my fist like a two-year-old, actually
tearing the paper as I wrote, "What do you want me to
fucking do?" I was angry at God for not being clearer. As
I look back, was God not being clear, or did I not want to

hear what was being said? Was God not speaking, or was I not listening? Asking these questions can bring up stuff we don't want to hear. I didn't. Hearing and reading this can many times take us to a dark place. We should live our life in joy, but this is important stuff. We have to greet this world with joy and not get too overcome in our own drama. Oscar Wilde said, "Life is far too important a thing ever to talk seriously about it." I think he was right. But as Thoreau said, "If one advances confidently in the direction of his dreams, and endeavors to live the life which he has imagined, he will meet with a success unexpected in common hours." (I promise those are my last author references for a while.) Sometimes going toward your dreams means sticking to them, and sometimes it means creating new dreams.

I have a belief that deep down—*deep* down—we know. We know what to do. But it is like letting go of one trapeze to grab another. We are scared to let go. Yet I truly believe to my bones that it is in this very action that God, the Holy Spirit, the universe—however you understand that power to be—reaches out to grab us. There is a Zen saying that goes, "Leap and the net will appear." That saying has proven itself true enough times in my life that I have to believe it. Everything we think is safe is risky, and everything we think is risky is the safe road. Do you want to be that guy or girl who played it safe?

Whichever path scares you to death, take that one. You have the rest of your life to sell insurance.

DREAMS IN THE REAR VIEW

I don't wish lousy shit to happen to anyone, but it does kind of slingshot you into purpose. Either it helps you acknowledge that where you are isn't working, or it helps you double down and work even harder.

After years of crappy jobs, the riots, and the earthquake, the lousy finally overrode Jay Leno, the Improv, *Days of Our Lives* (I was an extra), Dick Clark, the Hollywood sign, Sunset Boulevard, and "living the dream"—just barely. I knew that if I continued, I might break through (Woody Allen says 90 percent of success is showing up), but I don't know if my marriage would have survived.

The cost was too great. It was time to leave.

It was one of the hardest views I ever had to take in: the city of Los Angeles in my rearview mirror. I had called it quits. I wasn't leaving the city, or even the career. I was leaving the dream. The time had come when I had to give up my dream of stardom and late night talk shows and to start down a new road. Laura was in the car in front of me. I cried for miles.

What do you do *after* your dream crashes and burns? How do you pick up the pieces and move on? How do you regroup and build new dreams? It took me decades.

When you watch the dream crashing down, you want to do a number of things. It's easy to get bitter and resentful. It's really easy to make excuses, to have a hundred thousand reasons why it didn't work: "They didn't understand me," "I couldn't find the right people for my project," "Other people don't care as much as I do," and my personal favorite, "Other people are idiots." There are always a hundred million people to blame: your parents, your brother, your sister, your friends, your roommate, your boss, your agent, the studio, the seminary, the bishop (this one is very popular in my current profession). And the kicker is that you are probably right—to a degree.

One of the hardest things to grasp, at least it was for me, is that it is almost never any one thing. It probably was your agent's fault—to a degree. It was your parents' fault—to a degree. It was your boss's fault—to a degree. You know what else? It was your fault—to a degree. A lot of factors play a part in any success or failure. You have to hit the wave of life just right. That is often damn near impossible. If you have a big dream, the number of things that have to hit just right to make it happen is astronomical.

Which brings me to what no one wants to admit: luck. We hate the idea that luck plays a factor. But it's true. Ask anyone who has hit a certain level of celebrity, and they will almost never deny this. But it isn't just the George Clooneys and Ellen DeGenereses of the world. It happens in every line of work. It's why some people get the promotion, the new opportunity. It just lined up for them that time around. They hit the wave just right.

When I got cast in the movie *Dutch*, I called my dad to tell him the news. I was so excited. I remember very clearly his telling me, "Remember this. Remember this feeling because there will come another time when you *won't* be the one they pick, and you will forget about this ever happening." It wasn't the response I expected, but he was right.

The faith community I started, AfterHours Denver, could not have happened the year before it did—or two years after. Either we had the money and not the leadership, or we had the leadership and the money but not the right location. Or . . . or . . . or. It was the right people, and the right money, and the right timing, and tenacity, and sheer, stupid luck.

More often than not, those things don't line up. And the dream subsides. It sucks. And it's painful. I don't know how to make it right, but I do know you have to give it time. You have to grieve it. We think nothing of grieving a death or even a job loss, but a dream? Yep. We go through all the stages of grief: denial, anger, bargaining, depression, and acceptance. I lived in these stages for a long time—in some cases for *years*. I lived in anger and depression for so long I should have changed my mailing address. Now to be clear, I don't endorse living *in* any of these stages, but I do endorse some brief visits. It is only when you don't go through all five that they tend to rear their head again later, and that's an even bigger bitch. Go to them, go through them—just don't set up residence.

Now before I make it sound like I was a starving artist, telling jokes on the street corner for change, I am proud of what I did accomplish. I performed in front of more than a million people *before* I moved to L.A. After the move, I did television, a movie, and radio. I stood on stage weekly at arguably one of the hardest stages in the country during arguably one of the most highly competitive time periods in comedy history. I earned my living performing for years, made six figures doing it, and had a blast. It doesn't sound like a broken dream when I look back on it and put it in print. But dreams don't have logic on their side.

I got nowhere close to achieving my dreams. And I felt like a failure for years.

Not valuing your own self-worth is a sad state to be in. It happens when we confuse what we do with who we are. This does not just happen with entertainment types. It happens with CEOs and athletes, doctors and lawyers, and moms and business owners. It happens *a lot* with clergy.

THE KOOK

Laura and I pulled the trigger and moved to Orlando. Orlando was starting to explode in the entertainment business. People were calling it "a second L.A." Nickelodeon had studios down there, and there were a number of cable shows that taped there. I could still try to do warm-ups for shows, and with Laura and I both having worked in the amusement park industry, we knew there might be *some* entertainment opportunities floating around. I wasn't ready to *completely* give up the ghost.

With my tail firmly between my legs, I figured I could at least get a job doing the thing I knew that I knew how to do. Bartending always made me good money, and I got to talk with people, which I was good at. People would open up and tell me things they didn't tell their best friends, wives, or pastors. And I liked hearing their stories. I realized it was kind of like having my own talk show (the ultimate dream), only instead of getting Brad Pitt to tell me his darkest secret, it was Chuck from the shoe store at the mall. In hindsight, I realize I learned more about listening during those thousands of hours behind the wood than I ever did in pastoral care classes in seminary. Here was a skill I was developing that I didn't even know I was developing.

I did know this: At about this point in my life, I never wanted to pick up a mic again.

That lasted about a week.

Laura managed to get a job with Walt Disney World within three days of moving to Orlando. I applied at a nightclub called the Laughing Kookaburra Good Time bar (aka "the Kook"). I was trying to get a bartending gig, but as it turned out, the manager there was a comedy fan, saw the

Improv on my resume, and was impressed. He offered me a job being the entertainment and marketing coordinator and club DJ. It was even better money than I would have made as a bartender, so I jumped at it. The club DJ part was more that of an emcee than a DJ. I was to open the club at 4:00 p.m. and work until 10:00. The nighttime DJ would come in at 8:00, and we would work together for a few hours before it became strictly a dance club. My primary focus was to do giveaways, contests, trivia, and "Name That Tune" to keep people around and drinking until the club got packed. We had a buffet, and the games went over big, so we kept growing and growing. It was a blast, and they were *paying* me.

The marketing part of the job consisted of handing out flyers all over town promoting the club. I drove a god-awful lime green and orange Econoline van with a giant bird on the side. It was humiliating, but I was very used to that by now.

One of the moneymakers we came up with for the club was a weekly bikini contest. This brought in huge crowds, but we had to make sure the contestants were amazing. One thing a lot of people don't know is that besides Disney, Universal Studios, and Sea World, Orlando also has a significant number of strip clubs. One place where you can find women who aren't embarrassed to walk around in a two-piece is a place where they walk around in half that.

As a result of this, part of my job was to drive the "Kook Van" around town to all the topless clubs, drop off flyers, and try to convince the girls to come and make some easy money in our bikini contest on their off night. This is one of those times when the job sounds much better than it actually was. The van had no air-conditioning, I was always a sweaty puddle, and I had to wear a uniform of khakis and a lime green polo. I was seriously hot, and not in the good way.

Despite all that sweating, it worked like a charm. We packed the place, and everybody was happy. I was working from two to four in the van and from four to ten in the club and having a ton of fun. Probably too much fun.

The staff was very close and liked to party. It was not unusual for me to stay after I got off, have "a few" drinks, and leave at dawn. We all enjoyed the time we were having. Laura went to bed early because she had to get up early, our son Hudson hadn't been born yet, and I lived less than a mile from work. I did *so many* stupid things back then that I thank God every day that I made it through to today. We were definitely a staff that liked to work hard and play hard. I found out later that some of the staff played harder than others. It turned out that we had a lot of drugs being dealt out of the club right under my eyes, but I was completely clueless. I learned about this years after I left, but the clues had been right in front of me. (I always thought it was strange that one of our bar-backs was able to fly back to his home in Bogota every year for a month. Where did he get the money to take a month off *every year?*)

At this point, I was going every week to a United Methodist church in town, and it was fine, even enjoyable. Laura and I knew what we needed. She needed a good choir, and I needed a good preacher. One of those is hard enough to find, but both of them? At the same church? Not easy.

The church was fine. But honestly, I didn't think much about it. I never had a beef with church; it just seemed boring and irrelevant, and the guilt of not going wasn't strong enough to keep me going, so I stopped. I figured if this God was as unconditionally loving as everyone said God was, then missing a few days, weeks, or months (or years) wasn't going to set God off. I didn't have too many deeper thoughts than that about God. At that point in my life, it was like asking, What do you think about the color blue? How do you really feel about it? I didn't give it much thought, actually. I think I was like a lot of people who live their lives day in and day out without religion. It is just something that doesn't pop up in their mind much. It does when they want a job or someone dies or someone is sick, and they don't see any hypocrisy in that because they don't think God *needs* us to always be thinking about him.

When we started going to St. Luke's United Methodist Church, I actually enjoyed it. The pastor was super normal and a great speaker. I pretty much assumed that was about it. We would go to church on Sunday, get our dose of God, and go back to our lives. We did this week in and week out. Church was something I consumed. I went and *took* it. I *took* the sermon, I *took* the music, I *took* the classes and small groups. The church was a purveyor of religious goods and services. We gave the church our offering; the church gave us the goods. (I think this is where 80 to 90 percent of congregations are, and most pastors are probably okay with it.)

Looking back, I don't think I had any idea that that church, and particularly Pastor Bill, was about to change the course of my life forever.

ON THE ROAD WITH DAVE

Within three weeks of my time working for the Laughing Kookaburra, I was called into the human resources director's office. I had no idea why, but I was pretty sure I was going to get canned within a month of starting, and that would suck.

My time at the Kookaburra was fun, and it kept my performance chops up, although it almost killed my liver. I got to be on mic five nights a week and had full creative reign with pretty much anything I wanted to do. I was never crass, though. Even in L.A., I was never a "dirty comic." It just didn't ring true when I was on stage. For the most part, I am neither proud of nor embarrassed by my mouth, but being dirty didn't fit with my Midwestern style and my insurance salesman looks.

This was part of the reason I was so puzzled when I got word that the director of human resources wanted to see me. The Kookaburra was in a Disney-affiliated hotel, and we all had to go through Disney orientation, but there was no understanding that the bar would be a "family-friendly" joint. When I asked Jimmy the bartender what he thought was up, he said, "I don't know, man, but it's rarely good when you are called into the principal's office."

Shit, I was three weeks into this job and I was getting fired? Did I mention that would *suck?*

When the day came, I walked into the human resources director's office and tried not to be defensive. I had racked my brain trying to think of what I had said or done to get called on the carpet. I never cursed and never said anything off-color on the mic. What the hell was this about?

"Come in and sit down. Shut the door behind you," the director said. His name was Dave Mitchell. He was not only the director of human resources; he was also the vice president of quality control. I was *so* screwed.

I sat across from him and was scared to death. He was about my age but clearly had accomplished more and clearly had the power in the room. I tried to just shut up and listen.

"I don't want to be a director of HR for the rest of my life." It was the strangest opening sentence of a firing I had ever heard, not that I had heard a lot. (I'd had a lot of jobs—fourteen W-2s one year—but I had never been fired, except by *The Munsters Today*). His next sentences explained the previous: He loved training and presenting, but his job had turned into mostly showing up at litigation sessions for workman's comp and attending an endless string of meetings. He wanted to do something different. He wanted to focus on training and speaking. And he wanted to do it with me. I was listening.

Dave proposed that we form a strategic alliance: He would provide the learning piece, and I would help make it fun. It would be enter-*train*-ment. I was intrigued.

Safe to say, I wasn't fired from the Kookaburra, but now I had a second job. I would be getting back on the road, but this time with Dave and his new company, the Leadership Difference.

Dave and I are brothers from different mothers. I performed hundreds and hundreds of shows with him all over the country and even in Canada and Scotland. What was great about doing those jobs with Dave is that I learned to work in a million different circumstances with a million different clients. We flew by the seat of our pants many times. Sometimes we would figure out the gig on the plane, which used to drive Laura crazy. (Having been a customer service expert at Disney, planning and preparation were paramount to her.) We taught corporate clients how to speak in public in a two-day seminar that I still think is the best speaking training on the market to date. We also delivered a program in which Dave would train participants for a half-day, and

then we would test them on what they had learned with a
game show that I hosted. We had buzzers, lockout lighting, computers—the whole nine yards. It was about a year
before *Who Wants to Be a Millionaire* debuted. We perfected our shtick, and then when Regis broke big, we had a
great product to offer. We were traveling everywhere doing
a show we could do in our sleep, making a ton of money,
and having a ball.

We've forgotten more good times than most people
have had. It wasn't the Stones at Altamont, but we had a
good time—many, many times over. Having said that, we
never missed a single gig and rarely had more than wine
with dinner the night before a job. The night *after* the job
was a different story.

What I gained from this more than a brother was
my self-confidence. I left L.A. a pretty beaten guy. My
dreams were crushed, and I really didn't believe in my ability to entertain any more, let alone make a great living at
it. Between the nightclub job at the Kook on the weekends
and working the road again with Dave during the week, I
got my confidence back and slowly, ever so slowly, started
to see the light at the end of the tunnel. I knew I wasn't
going to be famous. In fact, there were days when I just did
the gigs for the same reason anyone does any job: money. I
was a whore. I knew this was the way I could make the most
money quick. I was making more in twenty minutes than I
currently make now in two weeks.

But in my heart of hearts there was something else at
play. I knew I had an ability to make people happy. Maybe
not knee-slapping, falling-down-in-the-aisles happy, but
I knew that people left feeling better than they did when
they walked in. I made them forget whatever was bother-
ing them, if only for a few minutes. In L.A., this ability was

being used for only one thing: moving me toward hosting *The Tonight Show*. Now with that brass ring gone, I started to see that the gifts that were moving me toward the late-night chair (albeit too slowly) could get me other places too.

I think that's true for a lot of people. We see a particular gift we have, and we frame it in the context of a certain job. Sometimes we have our breakthrough when we take those same gifts and drop them into a different box—not just one that we didn't think of, but sometimes even a box we didn't even know existed.

Obviously, I knew ministers existed. But that ministry "box" seemed so different from everything I'd been pursuing, it didn't even show up on my radar.

Oddly enough, the boxes weren't as different as I thought.

Chapter 5
WHO ARE YOU?

Ketchum Public Relations is one of the largest PR firms in the world. They have offices in major cities all over the globe, including on Madison Avenue in New York City. They are kind of a big deal.

Of course, I knew none of that when I answered the phone. I was in Orlando, but I was getting my game back. L.A. or no L.A., I was an entertainer, and all I knew was that any call could be a gig. I wasn't cocky, but I didn't know who they were, so I wasn't impressed either. I was living in a time of discovery, a time when I found my skills had value outside of L.A. and—I was starting to see—even outside of entertainment in general.

"Hi, Jerry. This is Carol McCormick at Ketchum Public Relations. Marc Summers recommended we give you a call for some possible work." Now *this* was cool. Marc was pretty famous in the hosting world, having done *Double Dare* in the mid-1980s and then tons of other shows following that. His recommendation meant a lot.

Laura and I had recently had our first (and only) child. I remember having Hudson in my arms, bottle-feeding him while I talked to the Ketchum folks. They were very nice and told me that it was a convention tour across thirty-eight cities. I would be doing a short game show on the convention floor all throughout the day, then

introducing the celebrity headliner—none other than Dick
Clark. They offered me more money than I had ever made
in a week for one day's work. I tried to act cool, but I was
high-fiving myself. (I am sure they were too; they later told
me they would have paid much more.)

The gig was pretty simple. I would fly into a city
on Saturday night, do the gig on Sunday, and fly back on
Monday—38 times. It was an awesome gig, and I enjoyed
what was called a "favored nations clause" in the contract.
It meant that even though I wouldn't get his money, whatever perks Dick Clark got, I got: limo, hotel, whatever. It
was sweet. I felt like a big shot even though all I was doing
was introducing Dick Clark around the country in malls
and other venues and trying not to trip.

I did two other tours with Ketchum the following
years: one with Gabrielle Carterris from *Beverly Hills 90210*
and another one with Olympia Dukakis, which involved
watching *Steel Magnolias* over twenty-seven times. (Ask me
anything.) Celebrities are an interesting breed. Some can
be amazing and generous and kind. Gabrielle even opened
up her house for me to stay in when I went back to visit L.A.
for some work. Her husband was as nice as she was. They
had their daughter's art on their fridge, and we all made
dinner together. She could not have been more generous
with her time and advice.

I worked with other celebrities (who will remain
nameless) that had outrageous requests and never said two
words to me even though we were working together. I have
seen celebrities turn down a six-seat limo and make the car
company replace it with a ten-seat limo, even though there
were only four people in their party. I have seen celebrities
demand that there be four bottles of organic merlot in every
green room across the country that they were in, and then

never touch it. I have watched celebrities return their water because it was too cold. This behavior stunned me.

Having said that, anyone can get used to anything pretty quickly and take it for granted fast. I remember one time sitting in a pub in New York across from where they taped *Late Night with David Letterman*. I was with a Ketchum rep who, at 3:00 a.m., after more than a few pints and quite a few Jamesons, told me she had forgotten to order my Town Car and would I be okay with a cab? Of course, I answered. She told me just to save the receipt and give it to her on the next leg of the tour. I was all smiles, but I clearly remember thinking to myself, "How hard is it to order a limo? Haven't you done this a million times?" I remember being pissed! I had barely ever even *been* in a limo before this tour, and now I was upset that someone had forgotten to book one for me. Outside, I was fine. On the inside, I was behaving like a total ass.

It reminded me how easy it is to get jaded to whatever we have, be it limos, a new car, or three kinds of pasta in our pantry. Charlie Chaplin once said, "The saddest thing I can imagine is to get used to luxury." We adapt and begin not to appreciate what we already have. This was a huge lesson for me: how quickly I can become entitled. I take so much for granted: a roof, air-conditioning, a bathroom. These seem like everyday things, so much so that we often forget there are millions in the world who have none of them. Many of them are folks you will pass on the street tomorrow.

There I was, getting picked up at my house by a limo, taken to the airport, flown to a new city, picked up by a limo, driven to the Four Seasons or the Ritz, going through the same process in reverse, and going to bed in a little condo in Orlando—only to get up Monday and punch in for my job at the mall. When your value is attached to what you do, this makes for a total mind screw. I was like one of those movies: librarian by day, hooker by night. It was a total head game.

Of course, the problem is just that: attaching my whole identity to what I did. There were few things that made me more proud than being able to write "entertainer" on my tax form every year. There was something great about sitting on a plane and when someone would ask, "What do you do?" getting to say, "I'm a comedian in Los Angeles." That brought me so much pride and satisfaction. Never mind that I was a *lousy* comedian. I was a comic in L.A.! Saying "I open for Dick Clark" wasn't quite the same, but it was still a source of pride. Lose that and what would I say? "I'm a DJ in Orlando"? "I work at the Gap"? I couldn't even have fathomed answering, "I'm a pastor."

WHO ARE YOU?

Some friends in L.A. once told me that in Europe you would never even consider asking people at a party what they do for a living. It is considered classless and shallow. Likewise, some friends who pastor a church on the plains of Colorado told me they learned really quickly that you never ask a rancher how many head of cattle he has or a farmer how many acres he owns. You might as well be asking them how much they make in a year or how much they have in their bank account. I never would have thought about that. It's just how we make conversation, right?

Yes, but we're also using the data from those conversations to help form our thoughts and opinions about other people. It's easy to make judgments based on these little slices of info. Does she have a cool job or a lame one? Is he successful or not?

I can't speak for everybody, but I think I do this because I judge myself on that one bit of data. I really miss the reaction I got when I told people I was a comedian. Their faces always lit up. Not so much with "pastor." Now, people either assume I think like them if they are Christian (more often than not, that isn't the case), or they think they know how I think and turn away in disgust (they are often wrong here too). Many times I just say that I'm a teacher or corporate trainer—something safe that gets no reaction. But I do miss the positive reaction. We so firmly plant our thoughts of self around what others think. Having gotten only one book deal, I have yet to introduce myself as an author, although technically, I could say that. I can feel my old sense of pride welling up as I say it, though. I question if one book makes an author. *Author* is a loaded word, like *comedian* or *pastor*. Those titles come with all sorts of preconceived notions of who this person is in front of me. Yet we know that we are so much more than our jobs. We are more than agents, or car salesmen, or stay-at-home moms, or comics, or pastors, or mechanics, or ranchers. Still, with each of those, we paint a mental picture in our minds of who that person we are talking to is with that one word descriptor.

We also use that one word descriptor to form our opinions of ourselves. That's a dangerous game when we lose a job or change careers. This I know, for my life has told me so.

I have to continually work toward being the best Jerry that I know how to be. When I do that, stuff just seems to fall into place. I think part of that is that I am functioning at a higher level of "me-ness" and don't waste time and energy trying to figure out how it will be accepted by the masses.

This is ridiculously hard for a former entertainer, whose future performances *depended* on how well the current performance was going. What people think of you when you are a comic actually *does* matter, because their reaction is the desired goal.

Having said that, we know that the best comics are the ones who don't look like they care. They are confident in what they put out there, and as a result, that confidence brings us in. That confidence, in and of itself, was part of the attraction. I think we get closer and closer to that as we peel back what Thomas Merton called "the false self" and show more and more of our core selves.

But that is hard to do when we're comparing our true selves (the person we honestly see ourselves to be) to others' false selves (the image they are projecting out of their own insecurity). Photoshopped celebrities and everyone's Facebook photos showing their awesome vacations and gourmet meals (not the credit card debt and dirty house) create unfair comparisons and false expectations of what we should be.

As much as I know how unhealthy and, at its core, poisonous it is to compare ourselves with others, I still do it. I also am ashamed that I do. I could be wrong, but I'm pretty sure other people don't compare themselves to others as much as I do.

C. S. Lewis said, "Pride gets no pleasure out of having something, only out of having more of it than the next man. We say that people are proud of being rich, or clever, or good-looking, but they are not. They are proud of being richer, or cleverer, or better looking than others." Most of us are crushed when we are losing the competition.

The higher the expectations, the greater the chance of misery. They say that your sadness and depression come from the gap that lies between what you *expected* would happen with your life and what actually took place. Aiming for *The Tonight Show* was what really shot my happiness in the ass. *Anything* short equaled pain and heartache and sadness for years.

The only thing comparisons and expectations rob us of—and make no mistake, that is what they do—is joy. A Buddhist saying goes, "Cease expectations and you have all things." That's probably true, but just like following Jesus, it's simple—just not easy.

LIKE A DOG WITH A BONE

Maybe it's because I had no expectations of church that I gradually felt more at home at St. Luke's United Methodist Church. It was and still is one of the biggest and most successful United Methodist churches in the state of Florida, which wouldn't impress me except that it is also big of heart. It is one of the "megachurches" that is doing it right and putting those outside the doors ahead of its own members.

The pastor of St. Luke's, Bill Barnes, has the unbelievable ability to spot people he feels are getting nudged by the Holy Spirit, and, like a dog with a bone, he does not give in when he is convinced God has a hold of someone. Bill plays a long game—never pushing, never forcing; just gentle consistent reminders. It works—like Chinese water torture.

I felt safe talking to Bill. He always made time for me. We would talk for about an hour a few times a year. I would tell him my story and my pain and my current state of fumbling around and why I couldn't do anything

else—especially ministry, which Bill had somehow determined was my God-ordained next step. I still don't know
why he thought I was being nudged in that direction. He
never told me what he saw, but he made it clear he saw
it. Bill would always listen to my excuses, calmly smiling.
Then he would tell me why I was wrong and that I would
know when the time was right.

Seven years. It was seven years from the time the subject of ministry first came up to when I left for Denver to
begin seminary.

Once Bill had planted the seed, though, it gradually began to take root. I think I was in a Hyatt ballroom in
Baltimore, running down the aisle, screaming like an idiot,
kicking off my 736th game show, when I caught myself
thinking, "Is this it? Corporate game show host in a Hyatt
ballroom in Baltimore? (No offense to Baltimore.) This is
my life?"

To be honest, the biggest reason I didn't think I
should go into ministry was simple: I didn't think I was
good enough. I wasn't smart enough or "holy" enough.

"I like brown liquor, I curse like a sailor, and I look
at pretty girls. I am *not* the right guy for the job," I told Bill.

To Bill's credit, after I revealed my habits of curs-
ing, drinking, and looking at pretty girls (not all at once)
and making it clear I was not the right guy for the job,
he simply said, "Maybe you are just the guy for the job.
Maybe we need more pastors who admit they aren't
heroes."

Maybe he was right. Maybe we need more pastors
who will admit they struggle with the same things we all
do. Maybe we need leaders who will admit they are a train
wreck and limping along. Leaders who are just trying to

follow Jesus and don't know what they are doing half the time. Maybe we need clergy who are simply human.

Well, when you put it that way, I was suddenly the ideal candidate.

That was the first time I really thought that maybe, just maybe, I could be an ordained minister.

Chapter 6

SINNERS AND SAINTS

I have a tattoo on my left forearm. It is a Celtic cross with a scroll wrapped around it with Latin written on the scroll. It represents what has come before me. My grandfather was Jewish, and the scroll is a nod to the Torah. The Celtic cross is dedicated to my grandmother, who is from Belfast, Northern Ireland. The Latin around the scroll is a tip of the hat to my Catholic upbringing, and it has some of my basic theological understanding on it. It says *Simul justus et peccator*, which translates roughly to "At the same time, sinner and saint."

It's been my experience in these last five decades that people often either get too much praise or too little. I know homeless folks who are the salt of the earth and who would give and share and love unconditionally regardless of who the other person is. I also know a number of people who have gotten *a lot* of praise in their lifetimes (e.g., celebrities, public officials, clergy) who were basically tools. The homeless never get a fair shake, and the other group gets the benefit of the doubt more often than not. For me, recognizing I am both sinner and saint is a reminder that I am no better or worse than any of my fellow men or women. We all have a dark side, a shadow side. God loves all of us unconditionally, warts and all. For me, the tattoo is a reminder that not only do I have a shadow side, but I need to acknowledge it and then forgive myself. It is a continuing process of becoming more fully human and living into who God wants and needs me to be.

THE CASE FOR BEING REAL

Having grown some over these last ten years, my concern about not being holy enough for ministry sounds silly to me now.

I do think clergy should, in many ways, be held to a different standard from those in the general population. When we are talking about matters of moral protocol and criteria, those instructing the "masses" should have some sort of bar they have to reach that is relatively high.

But there is an argument to be made for being a sinner! I don't use "sinner" in the traditional, conservative, Southern Baptist way. I see a sinner as someone who simply, as they use the term in archery, "missed the mark." These are people who made a mistake. They didn't get it a hundred percent right. They are off-center and off the mark. In that way, I am one of the greatest sinners.

Most Christians (and especially pastors) will admit they are sinners, imperfect, flawed—however they choose to phrase it—but they try not to let it show. Oh, they *say* it, but they rarely give examples. It's best if they can talk about when they *used to be* flawed. We Christians love a good redemption story. Author Peter Rollins talks about the fact that Jesus didn't hang around *former* drunkards and prostitutes. Maybe clergy are ashamed to admit their flaws (we all are to a point), maybe they think people need a perfect example to follow, but I think owning your shit can be as useful, maybe even more useful, when it comes to connecting with and caring for real people. Most of the drug dealers, hookers, and homeless people I see in the park every single week don't need a perfect example. They just need someone to love them without condition, without criteria, without motive—you know, like Jesus. Who the hell wants to listen to someone who is perfect talking about how right they are and how wrong everyone else is?

These days, I think people want real over anything. They want to see that you don't have it all figured out. They want to see that you don't have your shit completely together, that you struggle at times with your spouse or kids, that you are in debt like everyone else, that your extended family can drive you nuts, that you are bummed you gained a few pounds, and that, yes, on occasion, when nothing else is on, you will watch *The Bachelor, Survivor,* and *Say Yes to the Dress*. Perfect people are boring, and they have nothing in common with anyone else. Most of us don't like those people much anyway. I want someone who is pissed his car needs repair *right after* he just got his car back from the dealership for some other repair. Doesn't it make more sense to show people how we as Christians deal with the crap that the world throws at us rather than pretending we don't have any crap?

I think this is part of why it took me so long to go "all in" on answering this call to ministry. I wasn't going to pretend. I was going to bring my whole self to the ordination process and not beg to be accepted. It was about giving them my full self, and *then* seeing if they still wanted me. If they said I wasn't "clergy material," I wasn't going to argue. "Go until you hear no" became my mantra. If they didn't want me, I'd give them the peace out and go on about my life. Their no would be my sign from God that I was going in the wrong direction.

Life is too short to work to win approval. If you think you know, really know, what your plan is for life and then you find it changing direction, try to make that shift without losing what is essentially you. God made you a certain way for a certain reason, and honestly, if you change who that is, I think that is a disservice to God. If you have to change a significant portion of who you are to make it fit, I think you are trying too hard.

People see too much bullshit everywhere else in their lives. They want to hear the truth, even when it's messy and ugly. They want to see the pastor color outside the lines and screw up his sermon occasionally because *they* have screwed up occasionally. I read recently that the Amish deliberately will put a mistake in a quilt because only God is perfect. I love that. We should own our imperfections. Give perfection to God and accept yourself, mistakes and all. It took me decades to do that. I'm still working on it. (It would be weird to say that I'm perfect at not being perfect.)

Loving ourselves is really the ultimate challenge, and it really is where we need to get before much else can fall into place. Our greatness in this world in many ways depends on our accepting of our "ungreatness." Once we accept our less-than-perfect self, it is much easier to accept the less-than-perfect versions of anyone else. Then when we see those who are not deemed acceptable by society, we can accept them the same way we accept ourselves. This, to me, is the heart of grace—a grace that Jesus bestows on us. As we get closer to accepting our own imperfections, we accept others in theirs and in the process become more and more like Jesus, which in the end is the goal: to have the heart and mind of Jesus in action and thought.

When we accept ourselves as *both* sinner and saint and not one or the other, it can be easier to see others the same way, which is what Jesus did. The temptation to put people into one box or the other is a hard one to resist. I catch myself all the time doing it—and then I look down at my tattoo.

PRISON

Three hundred convicted felons are sitting in front of me. They are all dressed in those orange one-piece jumpsuits that are all the rage in correctional facilities. They don't look happy. Some look, well, hostile—like "say the word and I shall shank you with a sharpened toothbrush in the neck and make you feel like an extra on *OZ*" hostile. Not that I was judging. (Prison movies always scared the hell out of me.) They are silent and are waiting for me to say something to them with meaning, hope, assurance, and good news.

Sadly, this was the first time I ever preached. Ever.

It all started when I found out I was accepted at Iliff School of Theology. (It is not a *seminary,* and folks there are a wee bit touchy about that. I'm not exactly sure why.) I made the announcement to some "friends" at St. Luke's in Florida. I put friends in quotes because, well, see the next paragraph.

They said simply to me, "Well, you should preach here in Florida before you move to Colorado so you can say you've done it. After all, you are going to be doing it a lot." This was a fair argument. I will not say they were being deliberately deceptive, but I will say that when I got the date of my first preaching engagement and looked it up on my calendar, I was pretty sure they had made a mistake. The date was a Wednesday, and we didn't have church on

Wednesdays at St. Luke's. Surely there was a mistake. I will call them and get the right date, said that small, naive voice that is inside all of us but is not to be confused with God. That's a still, quiet voice. Very similar. This voice tells you stupid crap that you know deep down is wrong but you want to believe anyway.

When I called the person who had left the message, she told me that the date she had given me was indeed the right date. It was the date that the prison ministry team would be making its monthly visit to the local correctional facility. She said it would be good practice for ministry. I don't know what sort of "practice" I was going to get, or how violent the churches in Colorado were, but she did have a point—sort of.

I wrote a short sermon around the Apostle Paul's whole sinner-to-saint conversion experience. Prior to Paul's conversion, Paul persecuted Christians and even was involved in stoning Stephen. I figured that maybe the inmates could relate to Paul being a badass. It was worth a shot.

All the people I was going with had been to the prison before. They were part of the praise band. They were very nonchalant about the whole thing, like we were going to Grandma's—if Grandma were a convicted stone-cold killer. They told me that it actually wasn't that big a deal. We would set up in the cafeteria, which is right inside the first set of security doors, do our thing, and then head back out. Easy.

What I found weird was that as the day got closer, I got calmer, and as the hours went by on the day, I got more excited—like I couldn't *wait* to get up there and start talking. The funny thing is that many of the folks I came with did not feel the same way.

On previous visits (they were correct), they had performed in the cafeteria. But they discovered on this visit that that arrangement was just temporary. With a new chapel having been finished, we would be holding our service there. The chapel is, of course, inside the prison. Actually, it's much deeper in the prison—right outside the yard. We weren't in Kansas, or a cafeteria, anymore.

When we first arrived, we were told to empty everything out of our pockets: keys, money clip, wallet—everything. I was given a bright square card with a black number on it that I was to clip to my clothes—apparently so that if I got shanked, the prison staff would know that number 187's family should be notified to pick up his keys, money clip, and wallet.

After we were cleared of all our worldly possessions, we were standing in front of a giant steel door that suddenly slid open, and we stepped into a room the size of an elevator. Just as suddenly, that same door slammed shut—and I mean *slammed* shut. We all stood there for an awkward few minutes. Suddenly, a door on the other side of the room opened, and we walked through it.

We were standing in the prison yard. There were no long hallways, no other trick doors or elevators. One minute I was free; the next, I *really* felt not so free. One guard walked with us across the prison yard. Twenty feet from me was a guy in his orange jumpsuit lying on the ground shaking. (Come to find out later, he was having a seizure.) We kept walking and arrived at the outside wall of the chapel. As the guard approached the door and tried the lock, he realized he didn't have the right keys. He turned to us and said, "I'll be right back," and *walked away*. "Freaked out" is too strong a description of how I looked on the outside but not how I felt on the inside. We all just stood there for what I was sure was about three hours. If you had a stopwatch, it would have clocked in at about four minutes.

Once we got inside and set up, the prisoners were let in. I am pretty sure that none of them said, "Oh my God! That guy who is going to seminary and has never talked about God in front of people is preaching! We simply can't miss this!" I am also pretty sure that *any* excuse to get out of your cell is one that is welcomed.

There was one guard in a raised booth in the back who looked bored. (Wake up dude! I don't want to get run through with a sharpened spoon handle while you are dozing off!) He had one giant red button in front of him. That was it. No weapon, nothing else. In retrospect, I am sure that if he had *hit* that button, all kinds of crazy law enforcement hell would have rained down on that little chapel, but at the time, it freaked me out.

Here is the weird part: I couldn't wait to get up there! I could not wait to start talking to the inmates. Never in all my performing days did I have that feeling. It really did feel *different*.

I told them what a bad guy Paul was—how *they* would have crossed the street if they saw Paul coming back in the day. He was a bad dude, just like them. People were scared of him, just like them.

Then I told them *he changed*. A man who persecuted Christians became their biggest supporter in history. I told them that if it could happen to Paul, it could happen to them. I told them that with God anything is possible. Anything. I told them that God loves them right where they are *and* that God wants them to be the best version of themselves they can be. They were loved by God *right now, today*. And with God's help, they can be the best version of themselves the world would ever know, even if that still includes bits of the sinner. That is some of the best news: God takes us while we are a hot mess, total train wrecks— because the truth is, no one is a *total* train wreck. We all have that saint trying to come out—and that sinner pulling us back. Søren Kierkegaard said, "God creates out of nothing. Wonderful you say. Yes to be sure, but he does what is still more wonderful: he makes saints out of sinners." That is Paul's story. That is my story. That is all of our stories. And I decided that day that that would be the story I would preach from that point on.

After I was done preaching, I said my "amen" and sat down. Then something happened that kind of freaked me out. They started to stand up. They gave me a standing ovation.

It has never happened since.

I am absolutely convinced it was the Holy Spirit that got the standing O. It was also the first time that I knew— *knew in my bones*—that this was going to be my new job.

And that freaked me out the most.

PASTOR-IN-TRAINING

Imagine you are the fat kid in gym class. Some of you, like me, may recall this from experience. You are told to climb the rope and that you will be graded on it. You try and fail, and that failure is burned into your memory forever. If you weren't that kid, good for you. Those of us who were? We don't like you very much. It's that awful feeling of having to do something that you know you aren't good at, but you have to do it anyway. Now imagine that this happens every day for three years.

That was seminary for me.

It was not the seminary's fault. My nonseminary seminary was just doing and valuing what it does best. It just so happened to include none of the things I am good at.

I had spent years cultivating skills such as having good hair, wrinkle-free clothes, and polished shoes. A number of students at Iliff didn't even wear shoes. When they did, they would kick them off as soon as they sat down at their desks. While I was always (and continue to be) proud of my socks, I would never dream of doing this.

Critical thinking was the skill set they were trying to develop at Iliff. I was more used to making my point with a funny word or inflection, occasionally a goofy face. None of these were valued at seminary. In many cases, they were even frowned upon. Come to think of it, almost every skill I had tried to cultivate in the previous twenty years was of almost no value. No one cared if I could make people laugh, knew how to network, presented myself well, and worked hard to be likable. My whole persona truly became a detriment.

On top of that, entertainer in L.A. and grad student could not be farther apart in their skill sets. If you are trying to make it in L.A. in entertainment, mastering small talk, trying to be charming, being reasonably funny (even if you aren't a comedian), being able to network, and having the ability to adapt to your surroundings are all skills that are necessary to climb the ladder. In seminary, you need to read and write good. Prior to seminary, I couldn't get through an issue of *People* magazine. Social skills aren't just unnecessary—they are sometimes frowned upon. If you are too good at being social, you are seen as lacking depth or intelligence. Your ability to innovate is almost completely rendered useless. (Ironically, several years after I graduated, I received Iliff's Innovation in Ministry award; it was the first one the school ever gave out.)

In many ways, I had to almost completely change my personality to survive seminary. None of the skills that served me well in Los Angeles were of any use when I was in graduate school. I didn't even tell anyone what I did in "my previous life" for my whole first semester at Iliff. I was worried I would never be taken seriously. (Granted, an odd concern for a comedian, but not so odd for a student.)

I remember one time my Methodist history professor, Jean Miller Schmidt, saw me in the hall right after I had received a C on one of the papers from her class. I was pretty wrecked. It was still early in my graduate studies, and I was actually proud of that paper.

Jean approached me and asked how I was doing. I said I was really disappointed in the grade I got on the paper. She asked to see it. She then said, "Oh yes, my TA graded that one." I remember thinking, "This is great news! She didn't even grade it herself! Maybe I can get the grade changed." She then said, "Yes, he told me he could hear your voice through the whole thing." I thought "Perfect!" and told her so. She said, "No, not perfect. We don't want to hear your voice. We want to hear a thoughtful, critical argument on why you feel the way you do and ideas and hypotheses that support your claim. Your voice is secondary." I could see my shiny new grade slipping away.

I told her, "I thought the purpose of seminary was to prepare me to pastor a church and be a minister. I thought a huge part of that was to be able to convey knowledge to the masses that I learned in seminary and to be able to do that in a way that is easy to understand and live out?" I'd spent two decades learning to write comedy in a way that *didn't* sound like I had written it down. Now I was coming to school to learn to write in a way that doesn't sound like I talk so that I can get the degree I need to be a pastor in the real world, where I'll have to unlearn all of my seminary writing style and relearn how to write like a person talks. Jean looked at me, smiled, and said, "Jerry, you are going to make a wonderful pastor and preacher, but seminary might be a challenge for you."

Truer words have rarely been spoken. At least the second half.

Oddly, once I graduated and was actually doing the job of ministry, I found a number of transferable skills. Pastors need to be good at meeting new people, something I really enjoy. I was pretty good at adapting to different social contexts, whether it was a black-tie fund-raiser or hanging out with the homeless. Humor was useful in getting the message across during sermons, and the listening skills I learned during thousands of hours behind the bar helped in pastoral care.

I guess in hindsight, you always see it. You see the clues, the telltale signs. Ministry is a people profession, and I'm a people person. Still, I was hesitant the entire way. To be honest, I still am.

I still don't think I'm pastor material. I have too much of a love/hate relationship with the church. I have days when I desperately miss entertainment. I suck at so many of the skills that make up a good pastor. I couldn't name ten hymns with a gun to my head. I get cranky easily, especially if I don't eat. I love too much material stuff: clothes, food, good wine and bourbon (okay, and tequila). My prayer life is usually crappy. Why would God want *me* to do this gig?

Then I remember: God always picks train wrecks to lead the church. *That way* the glory can truly be given to God. That's what I believe, and if it's true, then I'm your guy! Zealots, tax collectors, smelly fishermen, murderers, and cheats—they all made up the motley crew that Jesus gathered together, saying, "Yeah, you'll do." Simon was a Zealot. The Zealots did not have a problem confronting any problem directly, as in "Let me plunge this knife into your kidney" directly. They rebelled against Rome with force. The fact that Simon never shanked Matthew the tax collector (a sellout to Rome) is stunning. I am certain at least one of the other disciples was constantly breaking up fights between the two. Based on the job description and the actions of the disciples, it is clear they were men who, as Disney's HR department would say, have many "growing edges" and "areas of opportunity." These are the models we have to work with as followers of J. C.

WHATDYA GOT?

How many people are held back from following Jesus by this mistaken idea that you have to have all your shit together to do something for God? Besides, a lot of the people who *look* like they've got it all together don't really, and a lot of the people whose lives are a mess on the outside have got some things figured out that a lot of people don't.

Some clergy I know get every benefit of the doubt given to them and yet are some of the most mean-spirited, unthankful, and spiteful people I have known. And I lived in Hollywood! A total jerk of a pastor is ten times worse than an entitled celebrity.

Interactions I've had with homeless guys on the streets of Denver, on the other hand, have blown me away. People look down on them and damn near spit on them as they walk by, yet many of the homeless folks that I know are the most upbeat, kind, compassionate, loving people I have ever known. They just haven't mastered that whole rent/ mortgage thing. People you would think have nothing to give still find ways to give of what little they have.

One guy on a low fixed income brought me a jar of jelly he had bought with food stamps to help make the peanut butter and jelly sandwiches that our faith community AfterHours serves to the homeless each week. Another man, who is now off the streets but eats the lunch we offer to help make ends meet, pressed $10 in my hand and said, "Help the guys." No fanfare. No big production. Just selfless giving.

Sometimes it is as important to learn how to receive as it is to learn how to give. To take what is freely given is part of the lesson of Communion. One of the guys, Kevin, would pay my parking meter whenever he had the money on him. Here he was, homeless and living on the street, and he wanted to pay my meter. He told me once, "Jerry, I have so little to give, please, please let me give back."

A modern-day widow's mite.

In the first year AfterHours was serving Communion and lunches in the park, an older man came up to take Communion. He was so drunk he could barely even stand up without falling over. I told him, "This is a reminder of how much God loves you." He took Communion and started to walk away. After about three steps, he stopped, turned around, and slowly started taking something off from around his neck. It was a cheap, brown plastic string of rosary beads. He took it off his neck and reached out to put it around mine.

It was one of the nicest gifts I have ever received.

You can claim to be a terrible sinner while still putting on a good face, but the real saints, in my book, are those who know how messed up they are and continue to let their light shine on anyway.

We have created a false humility within Christian circles that I believe is off-putting to those not in the "religious world." Own your imperfection, of course, but let's not forget that God made each of us unique and special—just not any more special than anyone else. We all have greatness within us. We need to use that greatness for good.

And anyone can.

Chapter 7

ME AND CHURCH: LOVE-HATE-
LOVE-HATE-LOVE

Now that I'm a pastor, part of my job is to encourage people to go to church. Come to a weekly gathering where you
can pray, connect to God, encounter the holy. It's good for
your faith walk. It's good for you. It's good for the church.

Here's the thing: I don't go.

I started working in a church—Denver's largest
United Methodist church, no less—as an intern in my second year of seminary. I was in charge of the young adult
group—which had yet to be formed. There was nowhere to
go but up! I ended up staying at St. Andrew's for six years,
and being there on Sunday mornings (whether or not I had
a part in the day's service) was just part of the gig. But once
I left to work on AfterHours full-time and didn't "have" to
go anymore, I didn't.

What is even more disturbing to me is the fact that
I don't feel any worse for not going. As a matter of fact, I
like having my Sundays free. If recent polls are a reliable
indicator, a lot of people feel that way. Maybe you do too. I
know a ton of awesome people who don't go to church, and
there could be a hundred reasons why. We church people
have to own that at least for some of them, the reason is that
church kind of sucks. Most pastors and churches have to
try to do a lot with very little. It isn't their fault. Maybe they
need to do less.

WHAT'S IT ALL ABOUT?

Most people I know who don't go to church aren't looking for a lot. They want community, they want to do good—maybe help make the world a better place. That's kind of it. But it's hard to find a community that you like and that pushes you to live more like Christ—a church that pushes you when you get lazy about following God and that will also give you hope and hold you up when you're about to fall. It's not easy, and honestly, it's easy to give up. And that's just the people who are actively searching. Never mind those that have said to hell with it. Good luck with them.

For a long time I felt guilty about that. I realize it is not a reflection of my relationship with God. As my friend Dave puts it, most of the time I just don't like the delivery system. I realized that if I could create a perfect "relationship builder" for me and God, it would include serving the needy in some way, being lifted up when I feel like I'm falling down, and being cheered on when I occasionally win. It would also include the encouragement to be grateful and to give thanks for all I have. But I can't speak for everyone. I took an informal poll on Facebook asking what people want to hear pastors talk about. About twenty people answered, and only *one* mentioned the Bible. One. Yet that's where we focus.

Don't get me wrong. I'm cool with the Bible. I think it gives us a great blueprint for how to live like Jesus. I think the sad thing is that most people never move beyond looking at the blueprint to actually building the house (or in this case, kingdom). It's easy to *learn* about Jesus; it's hard as hell to actually start *living* like Jesus.

I saw a poll recently saying that the most important issue to people in my denomination is that the church be focused on creating disciples of Christ (39 percent of respondents ranked it as first or second in importance). One would think this is great news, until you read further into the report and see that the issues ranked near the bottom are things like poverty and children at risk (both 17 percent), and social justice (16 percent).

What the hell? We think it's important to create disciples of Jesus Christ—we just don't think that the things Jesus thought were important are important. That's like saying you want to learn to swim, but you don't want to get wet. You want to get a college degree, but you don't want to go to school. You want to lose weight, but you don't want to diet or exercise.

Taking care of the poor and those on the margins is a biblical imperative. It is in the Bible *hundreds* of times, yet we continue to ignore it. It sounds to me like we want the church to magically make us into disciples without having to do the work to get there. Either that, or we fundamentally misunderstand what it means to be a disciple. Theologian Søren Kierkegaard had a third theory, beyond magic and misunderstanding. "The Bible is very easy to understand," he said. "But we Christians are a bunch of scheming swindlers. We pretend to be unable to understand it because we know very well that the minute we understand it, we are obliged to act accordingly."

My understanding of the gospel is that Jesus wants us to be and to create disciples. It's as simple as that. To me, *disciple* is just a fancy church word for "follower." A follower walks behind and follows the leader, learning to do what the leader does. Discipleship is more than coming to a worship service once a week and telling God that God is great. That takes no more effort than just showing up. That does not sound like the balls-out commitment that

Jesus called us to make for him. In fact, it is the antithesis of what he told us. He told us to *die to self.* Holy shit! That is not just going and sitting quietly for an hour a week. Jesus never said to spend 1/168 of your week focused on me and telling me I'm awesome.

Here is just a sample of what he *did* say:

Do to others as you would have them do to you. (Luke 6:31)

Go and do likewise. (Luke 10:37)

By this everyone will know that you are my disciples, if you have love for one another. (John 13:35)

Love one another as I have loved you. (John 15:12)

If we love one another, God lives in us, and his love is perfected in us. (1 John 4:12)

"You shall love the Lord your God with all your heart, and with all your soul, and with all your mind." This is the greatest and first commandment. And a second is like it: "Love your neighbor as yourself." (Matt. 22:37–39)

I give you a new commandment, that you love one another. Just as I have loved you, you also should love one another. (John 13:34)

Beloved, let us love one another, because love is from God; everyone who loves is born of God and knows God. Whoever does not love does not know God, for God is love. (1 John 4:7–8)

At this point, a lot of us might be saying, "Okay, I get it."

But do we?

Going to a certain building at a certain time to listen to a certain person *talk* about loving people is not the same as loving people. And *saying* you love people is not the same as getting out there and actually loving people.

Somewhere along the line we have become people who value what we believe more than what we do. The challenge is that most people on the outside of our churches value the doing over the believing. As my friend Tyrone said to me one day in the park while feeding the homeless, "You ain't talkin' about it. You bein' about it."

Theologian Peter Rollins said it well: "What we really believe, the true belief, the heart of our belief, is not in what we say, it's found in the texture of our lives." He says on his website, "I need to work out how the beliefs function for that person." In essence: I don't care what you believe, I want to know how your beliefs function. I could not agree more.

A lot of people think the folks under thirty-five who come to AfterHours come because we do church in bars. No question—that might be appealing to some on some level. But most of the people under thirty-five who come to AfterHours show up in the park to feed the homeless *first*. It is not the service of worship that pulls them in, but the service of people. And it is not "works that get you into heaven" thinking that is pulling them there. Most of our folks believe in a God of such unspeakable grace that we are *all* okay on that front. They are in the park because when they look at the works of Jesus, they see a human being of radical, unconditional, loving action. Action leads. All the verses above ask us to take action, namely, to love other people.

It's about giving, not taking. Them, not us.

Don't get me wrong. I love powerful, connectional worship that connects us to each other and to God. And when there are times when we are broken, really broken—

like a-carton-of-eggs dropped-on-the-kitchen-floor broken—
those are the days when we need to get something from the
church: love, support, companionship. When our spirit is
crushed, that is the time to take. We have to have in order
to give. Giving is part of what makes us complete. If our
souls and spirits are crushed, we need to get those in at least
working shape before we can give back.

In general, however, I think a worship service should
be an event in which we hear stories about where the Holy
is showing up in the world, and by the end we are so jazzed
and fired up that we can't wait to get back out in the world
to be surprised by where God is showing up next! Such a
worship service serves as a type of missional outpost or base
camp where we go to get our energy and supplies renewed
so that we can *get back out there.*

This type of worship can't happen if we aren't getting
out there in the first place. The stories happen *out there.*
We can only retell them if we are present in the world to
experience them in the first place.

Sadly, even some pastors aren't getting out there
to serve because they're too busy serving everybody
inside the church. Churches tend to bog pastors down
with meetings or email or preparations for this Sunday's
service to make it a fantastic event that will *attract* new
people and keep the ones who have been coming, still
coming. I talked to a pastor once who told me he would
love to join me out in the park feeding the poor and homeless but that he had to get the newsletter finished. That
made me so sad—mostly because he didn't see the sadness
in it himself.

If we could free up the time pastors devote to prep-
ping their sermons, and making sure the choir is ready,
and leading trustees meetings, and figuring out the next

stewardship campaign, we would create the time for them to be in the parks with the least and the lost, to be with those who are hurting, to be in prayer and contemplation to reenergize themselves, *and* to lead others to do all of these same things (which they will do when they see their pastor doing it). I truly believe that if we give our pastors time to love people, people will follow suit! This is transforming for both pastors and the faith community. This is the work of building disciples. This will transform the world.

No wonder the church has somehow trained the public into thinking that the center of a Christian's job description is going to church on Sunday, followed by being on committees and giving 10 percent to the church. These are all really great. But they are just part of the *stuff* of church. They aren't the *core* of church. The core is loving each other, especially those who are getting the short end of the stick when it comes to receiving the love of other people. If we don't know whom to love, it's a simple test: Is anybody else loving that person? No? Then that's the one! Those on the margins, those with no homes, those who smell. Those with AIDS, those in prison, those whom others might deem terrorists. Here's the thing, though: the work is hard as hell. A damn few number of people want to do it. Hell, there are a lot of days when I don't want to do it but I am telling others to do it!

I have said more than once that following Jesus is simple but not easy. In many ways, we have turned that around and made following Jesus easy but not simple. We have made it ragingly complex when it doesn't have to be. I think loving God, loving people, and loving yourself is a pretty straightforward recipe.

And somehow, people outside the church seem to understand that better than church people.

This "new breed" isn't against *going to* church—
they just would rather *be* the church. They would rather
be doing stuff like feeding the poor, and taking care of
babies and single moms, and visiting prisoners, and being
kind to strangers, and loving the unlovable. That is the
way they view the gospel. For them, it's not about vacation
Bible school or taking a class, even though those are good
things. It's just that the gospel doesn't tell us to do any of
those things.

WHY DON'T WE CHANGE?

Are we doing things that we don't have to do and not doing
the things we should?

I am going to put on my callous, jaded hat now. I
know it isn't a popular thought, and I know I will get some
arrows shot at me for saying it, but I think it is at least in
a small way—and maybe a big way—the reason we are so
scared to lose our members.

They give us money.

The church worship service is the ideal vehicle for
collecting money. It provides us a theological reasoning
(tithing) and makes us feel guilty when we don't give.

Compare that with what would happen if every
Sunday millions of people went out into communities all
over the country to service their fellow men and women,
specifically, those in need. I mentioned earlier that I had
read there are 100 million people in this country who go to
church every week. Can you imagine what kind of change
we could effect if we offered up to God not our thanks, or
our concerns, or our songs, or our prayers, but instead one

hour of service to those in need *anywhere* in our lives: the neighbor who is a shut-in, the soup kitchen downtown, the kid who needs help with homework, the elderly person who needs help with groceries?

One hundred million service hours—*a week*. We could change the world.

But I don't know how we would collect the offering.

I posed a question on Facebook recently: "Is the church of the future going to be a revenue stream for the poor and needy? Did Jesus ever intend it to be anything other than that?"

I was surprised by the pushback I got. I think there is a contingency (read: the institution and clergy in many cases) that likes the current setup. There are many who value their buildings and programs and full-time pastor status—the things that most of that money goes toward. I think part of the problem with the way things are being done now is that *so* much money is going to institutional maintenance that the marginalized are still receiving the short end of the stick.

In essence, is there a way to "do church" cheaper? Can we assist the poor and those on the margins in a way that gets more money to those truly in need and less to all those along the way?

And make no mistake: I get that I am part of the problem. Clergy almost always provide a huge strain on the giving to the wider community. When I entered into my fourth year of AfterHours, there was an expectation that we would be able to cover all of our own expenses.

Up to this point, almost all the money going to After-Hours in the form of donations went directly to the poor or to inviting people to serve the poor with us (coasters, bar ads, newspaper ads, etc.). By asking the faith community to pay for my salary, we are essentially asking them to give to feeding my family over feeding a poor family. It is a tough theological question to ask: Are clergy salaries taking food out of the mouths of the poor?

Now don't misunderstand: I believe in paying the workers their due. The question is: What are they due? Could clergy work be broken up into three roles: administrative, pastoral care, and teaching/preaching? What if a church had an office manager, a chaplain, and a preacher/teacher who each got paid an hourly rate? I've never been paid more than a couple hundred dollars to preach on a Sunday when I guest preach. Could day rates be the future? Bivocational pastors?

I have seen millions of dollars go toward things and not nearly enough go toward people. Don't get me wrong; I like things and I like beauty. It is just about priorities. I remember moments at St. Andrew when there wasn't enough money to help people who came to our door because we simply did not allocate enough money to outreach—and at the same time there were $10,000 pieces of art in our entryway. It is heartbreaking to know we can't help a family that is struggling, but we have *multiple* baby grand pianos. There is no question that affluent churches do a lot of good. It is rarely about one instance; it is a constant monitoring. When buildings get built and Jumbotron screens get hung while people lose their jobs, benefits get cut, and furlough days get enacted, something is wrong. If we are spending more money on sheet music than outreach, something ain't right.

They say your worldview can be different once you see how the sausage is made. I have found this to be true, and I bet that if you talk to almost any person who has been on a church committee or council, you will find they agree. Church looks different when you are sitting around a table at a finance meeting at 9:30 on a Tuesday night compared to when you are sitting in the pew Sunday morning. It can be really disheartening to see how different the church today can be from the band of followers Jesus enlisted.

But I believe there is another way.

Chapter 8

MICROBREWED CHURCH

I met my grandfather on my mom's side only once. I met my mom's mom maybe three times. I never met my dad's parents. Regardless, I know what kind of beer they drank. If they went into a bar or restaurant and ordered a beer, that is exactly what they did. They ordered *a beer*. No need to specify what kind, because there was only one.

Times have changed. Ordering a beer is an ordeal. There is not a bar, pub, lounge, watering hole, saloon, dive, speakeasy, or nightclub in the country or probably the world where you can go in and just order a beer. In my home city of Denver, that would be like going into a restaurant and saying you would like some food, please.

We have a few more decisions to make. Do you like lager or ales? Do you like porters or stouts? Sours? Flemish style or more of a Belgian? What's the ABV? Do you like a hoppy beer or one that is light and crisp?

For the love of Benji! I just want a beer!

When my grandparents ordered a beer, the bartender turned around and got them—a beer. Now we have hundreds to choose from. The market has expanded. Beer companies have expanded their market share as well. Budweiser has a ridiculous number of offerings. They do this because they know people's tastes have changed and they want more variety. There are still people who dig good, old-fashioned Budweiser. Hell, I'm one of them. I will still order a PBR more than anything (except maybe Guinness). I like my beer cold, crisp, and to taste like beer. Bud and Miller and Coors still spill more beer in a day than some microbrews make in a week, but they're no longer the only beer in town. Some people like Bud, but a growing number of folks are digging on Espresso Oak Aged Yeti Imperial Stout. Doesn't make the Yeti better. It is just different. The guy drinking PBR and the guy drinking the Espresso Oak Aged Yeti Imperial Stout both like beer. The beer folks have learned that in order to stay competitive, they have to be relevant to our times.

Sound familiar?

Established, tall-steeple, fixed-pew churches are like Budweiser. They work for plenty of people. But not for everyone. And the number of people they are working for is shrinking. The church needs to start thinking like a microbrew: offer something different. Not because you think it's going to be the next big thing; it may just be the next—thing. Starbucks has done pretty well for itself, and there are no 1,000-seat Starbucks shops. Smaller can work; it might even be what Jesus was thinking.

Another advantage of being a microbrew is nimbleness and the ability to change ideas on a dime. Big companies have long processes to change. There are definite advantages to being a speedboat when everyone else is a battleship.

I worked for a Budweiser once. Or maybe we should say Coors, since it was in Colorado. Make no mistake. There is *a lot* to like in churches with abundant resources to use. I don't know of another church that has such a deep commitment to adult learning and education than

St. Andrew. I would hold its adult learning program up against any in the country, in any denomination. We had a senior pastor who was deeply committed to biblical literacy. I believe the average congregant at St. Andrew knew as much about the Bible as congregants in any church in the country, and this knowledge went beyond chapter and verse. While I was at St. Andrew, we became one of the largest Reconciling Churches in the denomination. Reconciling Churches openly welcome gay, lesbian, bisexual, and transgendered folks. We had to vote on whether we wanted that status or not. The vote came in at more than 90 percent in favor. This kind of consensus on such a controversial issue is especially impressive for a large church. Large, traditional churches can be bound to "the way things have always been," making change and innovation difficult.

Ecclesiastes tells us that there is a season for everything. Are we willing to admit that there might be a turning season for the way we do church? Think of the evolution of musical styles. Bach could still get a gig today, I am sure, but he would probably be getting hired by Jay-Z. What once was the dominant form is now a niche preference.

One style of music is no more real than any other. But there are some styles I dig and others that leave me cold. If I like the blues but country does nothing for me, does that mean I don't love music? Does it mean I hate tradition? Does it mean I am attacking music? No. It means I have a deep, strong, true desire to connect with music, but in a certain form.

People have always wanted to connect with something greater than themselves, but we are discovering that many times the dominant, traditional forms of church don't connect with nearly as many people as they used to. As a result, something new develops. In the late twentieth century, it was contemporary worship music and a more casual theater- or warehouse-type atmosphere. It didn't replace the old, traditional style of worship, but it filled a new niche that grew and grew, to the point that (attendance would suggest, anyway) it became as much a dominant form as what came before. And now still newer things are meeting people in ways that neither of those forms of church are. And so it goes—and will continue to go.

I think when this happens, there will always be pushback. That is the nature of change. When Miles Davis and John Coltrane came on the scene and started to mix it up, purists thought they were attacking music. It took a long time to win people over, and even still, what they and lots of others did, many still don't dig. Even within a genre there are going to be changes. Delta blues gave way to Chicago blues, which gave way to Southern fried rock, which also had offshoots. You can hear the White Stripes do "Death Letter," but in a very different way than Son House did it—and that's okay. The Black Keys have helped revitalize interest in the blues again because of their love for the past, but with a nod to the present and future.

Church should be like that too. Too often we are looking for the magic bullet that will "fix" church. Does the church need to be fixed? Can't we just breathe deeply and see where the spirit is taking us? Maybe every church doesn't need to be in a stadium. Maybe that shouldn't even be the deciding factor for success. If the number of fans determined whether music was good or not, Justin Bieber and Miley Cyrus would be considered geniuses, and Bach and Miles Davis would be considered hacks. We need Muddy Waters, even if he would never have filled Madison Square Garden.

SMALLER CAN BE BETTER

AfterHours has been doing its thing for about five years now, and we've never broken a hundred at our gatherings. We're a small church, if you put it in those kinds of terms. We only do two things: We gather in bars on Monday nights, and we serve the homeless. It's pretty simple, but we make a difference by appealing to and including people who aren't interested in the typical, dominant forms of church as they exist today.

It seems that churches are trying to do so much, and often with very little in the way of income. It sometimes seems to me that we have a hundred ways to *learn about* Jesus: classes, book studies, curricula, Sunday school, retreats, VBS (vacation Bible school—I graduated seminary and didn't know what VBS was), pilgrimages, etc. But then to *be* Jesus? There are outreach and missions programs, and those budgets are some of the first to get cut. Our budgets show what we are really focused on. Sadly, I feel we are often focused too inwardly. ("The problem is that we are spending too much money on outreach to the poor," said no one ever.) We spend a lot on the stuff we do within the church building (not to mention the building itself), trying to get more people to come *into* the building and be a part of what's going on there. Get them in the building, get them to join the church, get them to write those checks—and we call them followers of Jesus. That just seems sketchy to me.

I find myself asking if we have made it easier to call ourselves followers just so we can say we have more people on the team.

There is a part of me that wants a smaller team— but one that's more badass, more over-the-top committed to doing our damnedest to live like Christ and not really caring if others join us. That would probably be a pretty small group. But as long as there is a desire to go out there and *love*, really love, then everyone is welcome on the team. We'd be like ninjas for Jesus, going out and doing radical special-ops-type acts of love and compassion. Rogue disciples, coming together to do extraordinary acts of grace and kindness—how killer would that be? I can tell you exactly how killer that would be.

Pretty damn killer.

More than once, the church has been seen as having an ego problem. *Sanctimonious* has been used a number of times. That's never a good thing, given that the idea of the church is to be a servant and not one who is served. Maybe at one time it had the muscle to back that up, back when Christianity was the "official religion" of the Western world, or when it was socially expected that you would go to church. But now, the days of the church being a thing that even has the juice to *have* an ego have passed.

In the end, this humbling may be a good thing.

If the church dies and is reborn in a different way, isn't that the story of resurrection? If we aren't willing to die to ourselves, resurrection is impossible.

If you know anything about Christianity, you know that the resurrection is a pretty big deal. Death is not the end; there is something beyond this life as we know it. It's kind of the point of our faith. Everyone is talking about the death of the church, and there is a huge part of me that wants to say, "So what?"

I am always amazed that the church is so scared shitless that it will die. Are we *really* scared that the church will die? Why? I think when the church operates from fear, we are moving away from God. I believe there is a natural evolution for the church. We need to trust that.

People get so defensive of their institutions. The very nature of a good institution is to be invested in constant improvement, to constantly change and seek best practices. So often the church seems to want to emulate business. However, it would be a rare business that would dedicate millions of dollars to a building that was only used one day a week for six hours. People will say that the return on investment on that space is worth it, but that ROI has been shrinking, and everyone knows this. We know the old models don't work as well as they used to. We also know the new models aren't going to work everywhere. (Not everyone needs church in a bar.) But by letting some things die and new things be born, we might find ways to connect people to God that the formal institutional church has never dreamed of.

GOOD NEWS

In the book of Nehemiah, there is a description of what a holy day should be:

> [The leaders] said to all the people, "This day is holy to the LORD your God; do not mourn or weep." For all the people wept when they heard the words of the law. Then he said to them, "Go your way, eat the fat and drink sweet wine and send portions of them to those for whom nothing is prepared, for this day is holy to our LORD; and do not be grieved, for the joy of the LORD is your strength." (Neh. 8:9–10)

What has happened to joy? Raucous laughter? Happiness? I have always struggled with the somber tone of worship gatherings. We have relegated the sacred to the sober. In fact, it is one place where I think the Southern Baptist Church and the AME Church have other churches beat! They seem to understand that resurrection—this thing we claim to celebrate and embody, not just on Easter but every day of the year—equals excitement, passion, joy. In short—life! Abundant life. That church that James Brown led in *The Blues Brothers? That's* what I'm talkin' about! They had it *down!* These qualities are essential for the church and yet are so often forgotten.

Somewhere along the way we equated proper worship with somber and serious worship. At AfterHours, we try to throw a party for Jesus! When we began, we took the time to ask ourselves, "What do we think Jesus would like?" We think he would like us to feed the poor. Check. We think he would want us to try and learn more about him and God. Check. We think he would want us to be there for each other and to really create community and all the things that go into that: food and drink and laughter and tears. Check, check, check, check. We are throwing a party for Jesus, and we want to please him. We think loving each other and loving those outside the "proper" circles society has made makes God happy.

My role as pastor is basically to be the party planner! Rather than the stern-faced scholar at the front of the room telling people where they got it wrong, where they have sinned (Don't we all know when we screw up? Do we *really* need a stranger to tell us?), I see my role as the one who is throwing the party to celebrate God and inviting people to the party. Jesus' first miracle was turning water into wine at a wedding. Far from just a magic trick, what if the message he was trying to teach us is that the kingdom of God is like the longest, best wedding banquet you have ever been to? That in God's plan, the food doesn't end and the wine never runs out? That is awesome! Wouldn't it be great to be a place where people could eat and drink and love *and* "send portions of them to those for whom nothing is prepared." That is what we are shooting for, people! Raucous, subversive, chaotic, sneaky love and joy!

I wonder what is holding people back from this kind of celebration? Is it the fear that if we aren't serious we won't take the gospel seriously? I can guarantee that isn't the case with AfterHours. In fact, I think the fact that we play hard helps us to work hard (for God).

Now to be clear, I am not talking about a crazy, drunken bash. Still, when Pentecost happened, people thought the disciples were drunk with wine, but they dismissed that idea because it was only nine o'clock in the morning. (Anyone who has gone to college or celebrated St. Patrick's Day knows that a nine a.m. drunk is not an impossibility! God *did* make Bloody Marys and mimosas.) Pentecost was about the church exploding in its style and look. It must have been a crazy scene. I wish I had been there. None of us were, so how can we recreate that, even in a small way?

Smiles and an easy laugh is a nice start. The power of a smile and its hundred and one uses continues to amaze me! It works on cops and homeless folks, bishops and bar owners, babies and those on their deathbeds. It is better than the Windex in *My Big Fat Greek Wedding*. It does everything, costs us nothing, and is a universally recognized currency. Those are some pretty good stats!

Yet it is completely underutilized. We are scared to use it. It is almost as if we are afraid that if we use it too much, people will think we are weird. Well, they would be right! And that's okay. I say, bring on the crazy uncontrolled love of a wild savior!

I think sharing the gospel is a lot more than just dissecting a verse from the Bible. It is telling people about where the good news is *showing up* in the world. It is taking those words on the page, blowing the dust off them, and showing how their ideas are being lived out on a daily basis all around us—constantly.

Most people wouldn't think so, but I take what I put on Facebook really seriously. For me, it has become a platform, a pulpit to a certain degree, to share good news. When I have good news, why wouldn't I pass it on to my 2,100 closest friends? When I share a story about God showing up in the world and I get forty, fifty, or sixty "likes," to me that is people giving God a high five. That is people saying "Hell, yes! There is some good stuff going on in the world." More and more people come up to me, people I barely know (yes, I will friend those I barely know), and say to me, "Your posts mean so much to me" or "I just love your posts on Facebook." I am certain they are not talking about the occasions when I post a picture of the steak and the Manhattan I am about to have for dinner.

People are *thirsty* for good news. And we *have* to give it to them. I have had some really crappy days, and it is amazing to me how easy it is to get pulled out of them just by someone who cares to share something wonderful or treat me with kindness.

I have realized that through the years I have slowly but surely let the world squelch my joy and happiness. I have too often tried to be cool at the cost of silliness and fun. I have too often reached yet again for a black shirt when a pink one would have been fun. That sucks. Too often I would rather be cool than funny. As a result, fun and joy suffer. I can't stand that. I have experienced resurrection, and people should know it!

It was less a burning bush transformation and more a clay-in-the-potter's-hands kind of thing for me. Somewhere along the way while I was at St. Andrew, I started to realize that I was in the midst of my own sort of resurrection, that I could bring what I had before my dreams died and carry them over into my new life. My previous life wasn't a waste but a prelude. You simply can't have a *new* life without a *previous* life.

I started realizing that the way I was able to make new people feel when they walked in my bar and my ability to put them at ease could be used to welcome them in a Sunday school class or special event at the church. I started to see that I didn't have to shy away from humor; hell, if there is any place that could use a laugh or two, God knows it's the church. Rather than hide those gifts, I needed to reengage with them—not to land a spot on late night, but to lighten the mood or to get across a tough-to-talk-about subject. Slowly, and I mean *really* slowly, I was starting to find my groove. I started not to be embarrassed about my previous life (there were those who definitely did not see the benefit of my being a former corporate game show host). Instead, I started to embrace it and offer it up to God to be used as God saw fit.

I am continuing to do this minute by minute. To this day, I am still not sure what the potter has in store. I hope it's a killer vase or a really badass bowl. I just don't want to be a crappy ashtray.

LATE NIGHT DREAM COME TRUE

I found I had a lot to offer in ministry, not least of which was the perspective of someone who had spent most of his adult life outside the church. One spring, my St. Andrews colleagues and I were in a meeting and brainstorming about how to get people, especially new people, to come to Easter services at the church. New people always come at Christmas and Easter, but we wanted to do something that would show we were trying to reach people in a different way.

I thought back to when I was a Christmas-Easter Christian myself. When I lived in L.A., if I went to church at all, it was for Christmas and Easter. It was over early, and I was left with the rest of the day feeling like crap because I was homesick and missing my family. If anything, I thought, we should do our damndest to break up the day so that it wasn't so long and sad for folks without family nearby.

I suggested that we do an Easter service at noon, followed by lunch. It could be something simple, like a chili bar with fifty kinds of hot sauce—something just weird enough to maybe attract the curious. Amazingly, after some grumbling about the later service, the rest of the staff bought it. We brought in a secular (read: normal) band that performs at one of those sing-along bars and pretty much knows every song ever performed. We chose all secular music that had a spiritual theme (e.g., "Beautiful Day" by U2, "Running on Empty" by Jackson Browne, "Prodigal Son" by the Stones). The service would have a short sermon and great music, and then we would move on to lunch. I talked them into marketing it in the free alternative paper, and we were good to go.

A couple of weeks before Easter, Susan, our marketing person, walked in and said, "Is the ad ready for

Westword?" This was puzzling because I didn't know I was doing the ad for Westword (yes, advertising in the paper had been my idea, but writing the copy?). She said that we needed to submit it in the next hour.

Well, that sucks, I thought. I decided I would just sketch something out quick and give it to her. Simple is best, right? I did a quick sketch of three crosses on a hill, a plus sign, and a bowl of chili, along with some quick text describing what we were doing. I did it with a marker in about ten minutes.

Susan said, "Looks great," and off she went. I didn't think about it again. We did our Easter chili lunch, which was well received. Done and done.

About six weeks later, I got a text from a friend saying, "Did you watch Letterman last night?" It turns out that our ad was on his show. I posted a request on Facebook to all my media/tech friends for a copy of the video, and within a couple of days, it was in my inbox.

Letterman was doing his rip-off of Leno's small town news, which involves riffing on ads and articles from papers across the country. He turned to Paul Shaffer and said, reading the ad verbatim, "And Paul, to wind up our stories, a church in Denver, Colorado, says, 'Come for the resurrection . . . stay for the chili!'" Paul kicked into his riff with the band to close down the segment.

Granted, I wasn't exactly on Letterman—but my material was! We got a lot of good buzz from that, and it was fun to hear about it from a number of people. (Hell, it's *still* fun.)

After Laura and I watched it, she just looked at me and stared. I said, "What?" as I often do when she stares at me. She said, "You see the irony, don't you? You spent most of your twenties and a good portion of your thirties praying to get on Letterman or Leno. You would have given anything. Then you quit trying, move across country, go back to school to start a new career, start an internship at *forty-one,* and *then* you write something in ten minutes that catches the eyes of the writers of Letterman, and it ends up on one of the shows you spent your whole adult life trying to get on."

Well, sure, when you put it *that way.*

God is never done with us. God always has bigger plans for us than we have for ourselves. For me, it took (and has continued to take) a complete release from my previous, personal desires. It has been about surrender, about learning to die to my old ways and desires (and make *no* mistake, they come rearing back all the time) and trying to figure out instead God's desires for my life.

I will not mislead you: Sometimes that new direction blows. It is full of hard stuff and lousy ways to spend your day. I cannot tell you the number of times I wanted to quit while I was in seminary (at least once a week), and go work a sales job. Or marketing. Or PR. For whatever reason, I stuck with it.

And every so often, at the weirdest times, when I think I am done and want to quit, God throws me a bone.

Chapter 9

CHURCH WALKS INTO A BAR

"If you are sticking around for church, great. If not, you need to put your drinks on the bar and get the hell out."

That was the call to worship for the first ever Last Call Christmas at Don's.

Cindy and Carolyn are two dear clergy colleagues who took me under their wings when I first got here and showed me the ropes. They also happen to be pretty good drinkers, lovers of those on the margins, and fans of Don's Mixed Drinks. Carolyn was playing golf with the manager of Don's, a bartender named John, and he asked if her church had midnight mass on Christmas Eve (the very fact he said "mass" spoke volumes). She said no but that there was a 10:30 p.m. service. He said that wouldn't work because he would still be at Don's. Carolyn told him that she could come to him. "Carolyn," he responded, "you do not want to be at Don's at midnight doing church on Christmas Eve." She said, "The hell I don't—and I know two friends who would want to be there with me." Thus was born Last Call Christmas at Don's.

Among all the staff at St. Andrew UMC, I always got assigned the last service on Christmas Eve, which was always at 11:00 p.m. We would do church, then light the candles at 11:55 and sing "Silent Night." It was one of the cooler parts of the job to stand up there at the front of the church and see all the candles lit up.

Afterward, I would throw off my robe, jump in my car, and head down to Don's, where Cindy and Carolyn already were. We would gather around the pool table, light the candles we had "borrowed" from the church, break bread, and do church. It was a short service: One of us would give an introduction to what the hell it was we were doing, someone would tell the Christmas story, and someone would introduce "Silent Night." The whole thing took maybe twenty minutes.

It is a good exercise to have to tell the Christmas story in "normal" language to people who, more than likely, are half in the bag. You have to keep it simple. We did, and it usually went really well. Usually.

One of the challenges that we faced and never quite mastered was the candle lighting. In a traditional church, this is one of the rituals we don't even really think about. The pastor lights his or her candle, then lights the candles of a few people in front, who in turn light the candles of those at the end of the aisles, who light their row. Simple. It is beautiful to watch the flames roll through the church like dominos, one candle at a time. When all the people know their job, it is cool to watch.

With a crowd at a bar like Don's, it's a different story. Many of these people were servers who had to work on Christmas Eve and came in for a quick pop before they went home. As servers, they were accustomed to—serving. When I lit my candle and tilted it toward the next person, most of the people there realized that the goal was getting these candles lit. At least ten to fifteen Bics, Zippos, and matches came out and lit the remaining candles toot sweet.

Fifteen seconds in, all the candles were lit. Not exactly traditional, but we made it work.

The magic of the night was not in the ceremony. (In my experience, it rarely is.) It was in the conversations afterward and the stories being told: three DUIs, multiple abortions, broken faith walks, and horrific tales of the church gone bad. I thought I went to do a service; it turns out that I really was there to listen to confessions. Don's may have been the location for more than a few shots and a beer, but make no mistake—that night, it was a church. I was standing on as holy a ground as I had ever known. I was blessed.

There is a special magic that exists in a bar at a quarter to three, as Sinatra well knows. Defenses are down, vulnerabilities are up, and people get real. Sure, some of that is the booze. But a large part is the fact that people won't talk to others unless someone is listening. If you are sitting alone in a bar on Christmas Eve at last call, chances are you might need a listening ear—not someone waiting for their turn to talk.

In some cases, you could tell people were bringing up things they hadn't shared in years. But they did to us, whom they barely knew. Their biggest disappointments, fears, and shame were pouring out on those early morning hours of Christmas Day.

A day that was dedicated to new life and the birth of a new thing was coming true in a sixty-seven-year-old dive bar at a quarter to four in the morning in downtown Denver. I firmly believe this happened primarily because we had come to them. Like the parable of the Prodigal Son, in which the father comes running out to meet the son, we were coming to them. It was these Christmas Eve nights that taught me an invaluable lesson: we can do church anywhere people are willing to gather.

AFTERHOURS: THE IDEA

I always liked church when I was Catholic. I never remember feeling particularly connected to God; I just liked the ritual of it, and I liked that I knew it backward and forward. I remember "playing" church, pretending to be a priest and blessing the elements. I just thought the whole thing was cool. I don't remember it feeling especially holy to me, though. It was like theater. It still is.

Here's the thing: Afterhours is nothing like a Catholic mass. I remember early on in the conceiving of AfterHours, I was very clear that the goal was to create something that I hadn't seen before and that I didn't know was available. It was not designed to be something "I would like." There already was a Catholic mass. I wasn't going to improve that.

I was trying to create an option for people who wanted to have a spiritual "thing" that wasn't too spiritual. I wanted it to be a service for people who wanted to go beyond talking and listening about Jesus to people who wanted *to be* Jesus. And I wanted it to be simple.

After being on staff at a church that, by all accounts, was thriving, I was getting a nagging feeling that there was a need for a different kind of thing. And by different, I didn't mean just sitting around tables drinking coffee with a praise band instead of an organ. I wanted to have something I could invite my nonreligious friends to and they wouldn't feel out of place and wouldn't get freaked out. It had to be laid back and have almost no church language. Even if you

had never been to a church service, you would still understand everything that was said and that was going on.

If it had a band, it would only play secular music.
I didn't know any Christian artists anyway. (I have since
learned that I really have been following a basic tenet of
Celtic Christianity that embraces the holy in everything and
not just in the church or on Sunday. There is lots of sacred
music that isn't "sacred" at all.)

I wanted to make a gathering that Chad and Dave and
John, and Irene and Ryan and Lindsey could come to and
think, "Okay, this is cool. These people seem normal
and aren't trying to push Jesus on me." That was the goal—
to make Jesus easier to swallow and more normal.

And at the same time, not normal. In many ways, I
think that has been the *problem* with the Jesus we have sold
to the public. In a nutshell: I think Jesus was a badass. He
was a charming, likable, passionate badass who fought for
the underdog and made *everybody* feel welcome—*especially
those no one else accepts.* We all have known that guy. The
guy who never started a fight but would never back down
from one either, especially if he felt someone was taking
advantage of someone who couldn't fight back. We all dig
those people. We all want to be those people—the doers of
good, the defenders of justice. We need superhero Jesus.

I think in most cases we have delivered meek and gentle and soft-talking Jesus. I think Jesus was fun! At the very
least, he wasn't against it. Hell, his first miracle was turning water into wine. How totally badass is that? And not
some generic box wine or two-buck chuck. Jesus turned the
wine into awesome, killer Brunello di Montalcino! 2006!
After the wine they already had had run out! Jesus wanted
to keep the party going. Was this a way to tell us what the
kingdom of heaven was like? A celebration that keeps on

going? *That* was the message I wanted to convey. An easygoing, fun, celebratory gathering where we enjoyed each other's company, gave thanks, and took care of others who couldn't care for themselves. This sounded like an idea that could catch on.

I sold the idea to the church council, and we did our first preview service in the fall of 2007. At those early Sunday night gatherings, I was really trying to create an "Ellen DeGeneres meets Oprah Soul Sunday" vibe, though I didn't have the language for it. We had a band made up of local musicians who worked at one of the piano sing-along bars—really *solid* guys who gigged five days a week in front of a live audience. They played music that was secular but had spiritual themes; think U2, the Doobie Brothers, and Jackson Browne (this church was mostly baby boomers).

When we first started as a ministry of St. Andrew, before we became our own separate faith community, people sat at tables—which sucked because we were in the sanctuary. We moved *out* six hundred to eight hundred chairs, rolled in round tables, and put two hundred to three hundred chairs around them. (That got old quick!) It was a mix of typical church stuff and more innovative things. I gave a full-length sermon. We had prayer stations, because that's what people were doing in alternative/experimental churches at the time. We had Communion, but we also created a new sacrament, where bread and mashed grapes became not just a symbol of God's love for us but of our love for the world. We made peanut butter and jelly sandwiches together and packed them up to serve to Denver's homeless the next day. It was a long way off from what AfterHours would become, but the sandwiches were part of it from the beginning.

We had over three hundred people at our first service. We did the next time too. And the next time. This made everyone very happy. It was all going great except for one thing. We were failing.

The goal of this service wasn't to get butts in the seats. It was to get *particular* butts in the seats—those people who would never otherwise set foot in church. We were filling our space, but it was with our own people. It was with the St. Andrew folks who didn't want to get up on Sunday morning, so they would wait for Sunday night. It was filled with people who had spent the weekend in the mountains and wanted to get one more run down the mountain before heading into the bumper-to-bumper traffic that is I-70 on a Sunday. We were reaching people alright. We just weren't reaching the people we *said* we would reach. Something needed to change.

Looking back on it, I can scarcely believe I did this, but I went back to the powers that be and told them that it wasn't working according to our mission and vision. Part of the problem was the very place we were in. All you have to do is mention "Highlands Ranch" to people who live in downtown Denver or even the surrounding suburbs, and people roll their eyes. Highlands Ranch is an affluent community. Add to that a new building going up on-site and flat-screen TVs and the BMWs and Mercedes in the parking lot, and you could see we were what many of the people I wanted to reach were raging against. Don't get me wrong; I live in Highlands Ranch, and I like it. It has a great school system for Hudson, and it is clean and convenient. (We own the smallest house in the community and didn't have air-conditioning for ten years, but we do indeed live there!) We needed to move off-site from the church. The question was where.

We tried what seemed like the perfect place: Life-Spot, an off-site coffeehouse that we used for youth events. It worked great—for a while. Then the rent got too high, and we couldn't make it work. We also tried the fellowship hall of another church. It just wasn't clicking. Something felt off. Looking back, I realize I didn't trust my own idea enough . . . some of it was "me": the upbeat party feel, the band, the tables . . . but some of it wasn't. The prayer stations for example. I've seen them done really well at other churches. I just knew, deep down, it wasn't "me" or After-Hours. I was trusting what worked for others and not what I was feeling in my gut.

It felt like we had one foot in the old ways and one foot in the new. That is a high-stress place to be.

HOLY SPIRIT(S)

After more than three years of doing AfterHours as an outreach ministry of St. Andrew UMC, I was appointed to AfterHours by our bishop, and it became my official gig. We would be funded for three years, so I didn't have to worry about finding donors or talking to people about money (is there any bigger turnoff to someone new to church?). I had stated in the first sentence of my business plan for AfterHours, "No building." This would not be the sort of new church start that meets wherever it can until it gets going, then can't wait to build a building. I have seen the cost of buildings almost destroy a church, and I haven't seen when the upside outweighed the bad. Don't get me wrong—I think there are a ton of churches doing amazing ministries that are in buildings, sometimes *big* buildings.

I just have seen the cost of those buildings really limit or even crush a church financially.

No, we would be a people without a home, like nomads, wandering from place to place. But where?

This brings me back to my ten years as a bartender. I would take time away and then come running back. You can't beat the money or the hours, and as long as you dig being freaked out with brain-numbing stress five nights a week, you should be golden.

I feel like I have worked for every casual dining chain in the country: TGIFridays, Olive Garden, Red Robin, Chili's (it is actually more depressing when I list them like that). To be clear, the food works for me. I dig sushi just like the next person, but sometimes you just need poppers, nachos, or potato skins.

I also bartended in museums, pool halls, and shitty shot-and-a-beer joints. I was, as they say, cut out for it. I sucked as a waiter, but I was a pretty decent bartender. I usually got the good shifts, but I worked my fair share of day shifts and the hellish Sunday and Monday nights. There is little to no money to be made those nights unless you do some sort of gimmicky thing to bring people in.

Like, say, church in a bar.

I pitched AfterHours in the bar to fill in a slow night at places all around town. I knew the only nights when we had a chance would be Sunday and Monday. It took months to find our first place. Things would start to work out, and then the deal would fall through. Finally, we found an Irish pub on Colfax, a relatively sketchy street in downtown Denver. The manager agreed to give us a try. He was a bit confused that we were going to do church *and* be drinking. I told him I could bring in twenty to thirty people. He agreed to give it a go.

I brought in eighty-seven.

Bar owners find Jesus right quick when you bring in eighty covers on a Monday night.

Of course, we didn't keep those numbers up as we expanded. With each new bar that we added, we cannibalized our own crowd because the new place was closer or cooler or whatever.

Having said that, people did have their favorites, and that was fine with us. Most churchgoers say they go every week but that's BS, and the stats people know it. The average *consistent* churchgoer goes about twice a month. If AfterHours can get *non-churchgoers* to attend once a month, I call that a victory.

For a number of people, the idea of doing church in a bar is uncomfortable. The blending of booze and Bible freaks them out a bit. (Some of these people are in my own family.) I completely get that. AfterHours totally isn't for them. In the same way, the church they attend isn't a fit for many of our members. Don't get the wrong idea—our members don't come because it's the only place they can drink. They are big boys and girls. They can drink a number of places. It is the relaxed atmosphere, the non-judgment, and the overall joy of the gathering that draws them in—in a way that traditional church doesn't.

I have found that the bars are more accepting of the church than the church has been of the bars. Most people's response when I tell them what we are is, "That's kinda badass." Church people are surprised to hear how open the bar owners and servers are to us. It makes me wonder if they've ever met any unchurched people. (I hate that term, by the way. It's so condescending—like someday they might be like us!) I don't understand church people who only hang around other church people. I don't read books telling me what the unchurched are like. I actually go out and meet my very own unchurched people—*every day*. Oftentimes I have known these people for years and they have never come to one of our gatherings, but I will tell you this: I have officiated at their weddings. I have baptized their children. I have sat and drunk with them and heard their pain after they have been fired. Make no mistake—I am their pastor. Proud of it too. They are some of the best people I know, and they haven't set foot in a church for years, including mine—and that's fine.

Another misconception about church in a bar is that people will be uncomfortable if they don't drink. Actually, a decent number of our folks don't drink. They come for the environment. (Almost all of the bars we are in serve great food. The ones that don't—you know who you are.) Drinking is allowed but not *required*. We have a number of people who come to AfterHours because of the nonjudgmental attitude of our folks. Drink or don't drink; honestly, they could care less. Judgment's a bitch, and people are over it. Judgment from church people is what drove most people out of the church in the first place.

We never encourage getting bombed. We stay within the guidelines of the United Methodist *Book of Discipline*, which states on page 108, "With regard to those who choose to consume alcoholic beverages, we believe in judicious use with deliberate and intentional restraint, with Scripture as a guide." (It is the one part of the *Book of Discipline* I have memorized.) I must admit that I find this funny, because there are some awful examples of booze use in the Bible (e.g., Noah getting smashed, Lot's daughters getting their dad loaded—the list goes on). We try to do *better* than the biblical example and stick to "judicious use" and "intentional restraint."

But to each his own, Noah . . .

We started gathering at a different bar every Monday, a marketing nightmare that everyone said was an awful idea, but people followed us (thank God). People have asked me a number of times how I got my locations, and my answer is always the same. Beer. I drank a lot of beer at those bars first. Don't misread that. I didn't get drunk. I would just pop in, have a beer, chat a bit, and go on my way. I sat. I listened. I heard people's stories. (It's amazing how much people will think you are a good conversationalist if you don't say much and listen instead.) You become a regular and let them see that you are "regular." You are normal. You are not going to ask people if Jesus Christ is their Lord and Savior or perform an exorcism on the bartender. Many times I will go into a place three, four, five, even six times before anyone asks what I do. I'm fine with that. I make friends. There are a number of places where I still go even though I long ago stopped trying to do After-Hours there.

After getting the first bar, it got easier. We had stats from the first bar to give the second bar. After we got the second bar, we got the third, whose manager happened to know the owner of the fourth bar and who basically called him and said, "Dude, if you want to boost your Monday night, you've *got* to get this church in your bar." We became a floating crap game for God.

We always made sure that the scenario was fair for everybody. They were not just doing us a favor. We were doing them a favor as well. We never paid a single cent to rent any building to do AfterHours in, and—here's the beautiful part—*everybody was happy*. The conference trustees didn't have to approve a building, the bar owners got to fill their coffers with cold hard cash, and we got a place to

gather to service the world, have community, and listen to
each other's highs and lows. It was a win/win/win.

One of our first spots was Don's Mixed Drinks (of
aforementioned "Last Call Christmas" fame). Many people
would call Don's a crappy dive bar. It is basically just a
neighborhood bar that has stood the test of time. I'd been
going there since we moved to Denver, and I knew the
owner, Ryan. My pastor pals Cindy and Carolyn and I had
done a couple of fund-raisers for the homeless in Denver by
guest-bartending there. We would tend bar in our clergy
collars for about three hours and donate all our tips to the
homeless of Denver. People would pay three dollars for a
PBR Tallboy, then throw us a ten and tell us to keep it.
(People are generous when they get to help people directly.
The money they donated that night bought food and clothing for our friends without homes the next day.) After we
had done a couple of successful guest-bartending gigs,
Ryan said to me, "Why don't you do AfterHours here?"
I hadn't asked because I couldn't believe it was possible.
Don's had been named the best dive bar in Denver for five
years running. It was a legend of a bar. To snag that would
be the Holy Grail.

Ryan and I went out one day, grabbed burgers and
beers, and hashed out the whole thing. We would show up
on the first Monday of the month and do our thing. In turn,
we would be good customers. Ryan and his crew let us
make our sandwiches, and a number of times patrons at the
bar would join in with us. That is always a beautiful thing.

Later, I was telling Ryan about how badly I wanted to
get on South Broadway. South Broadway had a great mix
of tattoo parlors, liquor stores, and dive bars as well as cool
clothing stores, nice restaurants, and hipster coffee places.
It would have been a great place to do an AfterHours

gathering. "Do you want me to call Alan?" Ryan said to me as he poured a shot of Powers and opened a PBR. "That would be great!" I said, not having the slightest idea who Alan was but thrilled that Ryan was willing to call this person on our behalf. Turns out that Alan is the owner of the Irish Rover, an iconic pub right in the middle of where South Broadway was catching fire. It would be a dream to be there.

About two weeks later, a man with a thick Irish brogue left a message on my voice mail that was music to my ears: "Hey Jerry, it's Alan over at the Rover. Ryan told me what you were doing with the church and the homeless. Brilliant, brilliant. I can give ya our new room the second Monday of every month; would that work for ya, Jerry? Gimme a call back and let me know." And that is how we got the Rover.

Not every place we tried was successful. Sometimes we crashed and burned. We would try a place one time and realize clearly that the staff did not dig us being there. That was usually a one and done. We knocked the dirt off our Doc Martens and moved on.

Sometimes they liked us, but it just didn't work. The second place that brought us in was awesome. The servers were great, the management was great. What sucked was the location. It was a couple of blocks from Coors Field, where the Rockies play, and whenever there was a home game, the bar would rent out its parking lot. I was not going to keep making the AfterHours folks pay to park, pay to eat, and *then* ask for an offering. It was just the wrong physical location. Such is life.

All in all, we have the locations we want, but they all started with me sitting at the bar and becoming friends with the people who worked there. It isn't just a cliché: in the end, relationships are everything. People know when they are being played, and they know when you are being real. The BS antenna of the service industry is finely tuned.

One of the best feelings I have in our gatherings is when we tell everyone about the offering pitcher that is sitting on one of the high tops, and one of the servers, who has just been tipped with money from one of our people, walks over and puts that money into the beer pitcher to feed the homeless of her community. She might not have much to offer financially, but the money she does give is hard earned. That is when I know we are on to something. It is palpable. You can feel it.

When someone who doesn't have much to begin with turns around and drops three or four bucks in the pitcher, I think that is kingdom of God stuff. Like a serious, hardcore, modern-day widow's mite kind of thing.

BATHROOM MARKETING

The plan was that you would be drinking in a bar, you would have to go pee, and you would learn about our church. It seemed simple enough.

That wasn't exactly the way I put it, but that was basically the marketing plan for AfterHours. It came about when I was first conceptualizing the idea for AfterHours and realized that if we wanted to get a whole different clientele, we needed to advertise in a whole different way. (Please forgive me if you are offended by business language and marketing terms.) I *know* my product is the kingdom of God, but I need to sell something else. Hell, even the term *kingdom of God* is off-putting to some people. We are selling people a feeling, an experience. We are not selling church. I don't

even care if they call it church. As long as there is service
and a connection to God and humanity, I'm good.

I was out one night and went to the bathroom to use
the urinal. I saw all kinds of ads in front of me: barbershops,
limo companies, DUI lawyers, Hooters—but no churches!
I knew this was a golden opportunity. I was constantly
looking for the ways other products were marketed to see
if that would work for us. Those signs above urinals and
inside stalls looked ideal.

I called the guy who sold the ads and asked him if
he had any churches. There was a long pause. "Uh, no."
(Interestingly, he had some in other cities but not in Denver.) We locked it down.

For the first couple of years our marketing consisted
of toilet ads and coasters. The coasters served multiple pur-
poses: advertising, business cards, free drink coupons, etc.
We only got them printed on one side so that the other side
could function in whatever way we wanted to stamp them.
We gave them to all the local bartenders that I had become
friends with to hand out with drinks. If the customers
asked, the bartenders would tell them about AfterHours.

That kind of marketing costs a fortune. To be clear,
it cost *me* a fortune. A lot of heavy tipping went into getting that favor down the road. The truth is, though, that
a lot of those bartenders dig our thing. Mostly because we
are pretty normal (actually, God knows, not normal, but
not—churchy). This is what I feel people are looking for
more than anything—other people who can just be normal
but still talk about God and do good works. No insider language, no special rooms or songs. Just normal.

My bartenders handed out a lot of coasters in the
early years, mostly on Friday and Saturday nights. Between
those and the toilet ads, people started to take notice. When

I'd hand people a coaster (aka my business card) with our logo on it, they'd ask, "Hey, are you the bathroom church?" As odd as it was to answer yes, I did it. They at least knew us and recognized the marketing.

At other times, people asked if we were "the peanut butter and jelly church." I would say yes to that too.

Part of our challenge was that we didn't fit snuggly into any one category. Some people thought of us as an outreach or a "ministry" because of the lunches in the park, but not a church. Others just saw us as a group that "got together and drank beer"—definitely not a church. We weren't churchy enough for church people. Others just wanted to make us a nonprofit and eliminate the gathering-together element completely. It honestly freaked a lot of people out.

I liked not fitting into a certain category. It made sense to me. We came together to have community to help those outside our community. The ads tried to convey that we didn't take ourselves all that seriously. The bathroom ads showed a picture of a hand holding a beer, a plus sign, the word *God*, another plus sign, and a peanut butter and jelly sandwich. At the bottom, it said, "Come hang out with us as we feed the homeless, drink beer, and talk about God. It's like church—without the parts that suck."

It got a great response—*outside* the church. Many church people, however, were offended. While that sucks for a people pleaser like myself, it didn't bother me too much when I reminded myself that *the ads weren't for them.* Those folks have a church. Blessings to them! Now move along. The ads were for the 200 million people in the country who don't have any place they can get together and live out the gospel. That's all we wanted to provide: a place to have community and live out the gospel.

I truly believe that people aren't tired of God. They are tired of the bullshit. They are tired of being sold a bill of goods. They are tired of hearing one thing and seeing another. They want transparency, they want authenticity, they want genuine dialogue. (I learned all these phrases in seminary. In the real world, people simply say, "Don't bullshit me.")

Isn't that what we appreciate in *every* relationship? Don't we hate the idea of being conned? We are sick of the church's bait-and-switch. We hate when we *thought* we were just having a conversation with someone casually, and then we discover that we were being played. *That* sucks. I don't believe Jesus would have pulled that shit. Jesus didn't try to trick anyone. And make no mistake, if you have a plan walking *into* a conversation, you have an agenda. I think, if your actions aren't enough, then your words certainly aren't going to convince them. Stop trying to sell the sizzle if you don't have the steak.

GOD STUFF

I was talking to a guy in a tequila bar I had wandered into while waiting to meet a bride and groom. We started talking tequila, and he clearly knew his shit. Suddenly, he started asking the bartender for half shots of two or three different tequilas. (There are *no* booze geeks as passionate as tequila geeks. They are always saying, "You have to try this!") After a few of those, we started talking beyond tequila. After mentioning that I had come to Denver for grad school and gotten my sommelier certification the same year I got my master's, he asked me, "What was your master's in?" I told him. He stared. Then he said, "Wait, like, do you have a church and shit?" Yep. I have a church and shit. I handed him a coaster, and he said, "Are you the church that does your thing at the Irish Snug? I just moved two blocks from there."

This happens *all the time*. I didn't walk in there hoping I would get to talk about AfterHours. I went in there for a drink. Next thing you know, I find a fellow tequila geek who happens to ask about what I do—and then we are off (and by the way, if we hadn't started talking about church, that would have been cool too).

I am stunned by how often I see "God stuff" happening all around me. I have a hard time thinking it just started showing up. There was a shift. I think that shift happened the second I started actually looking around and watching for it. When I did, I realized it was everywhere.

I spent my life running around trying to make something of my life. The truth? My life was already right in the middle of amazing things everyday; I just was too busy looking forward to tomorrow. In the process, I missed today.

God is right there, in the woman serving you your drink or the guy flying his sign on the corner.

Don't miss it.

Chapter 10
TAKIN' IT TO THE STREETS

Some ex-cons, dealers, hookers, junkies, and Jesus. The chronically homeless. That's who shows up in the park on a daily basis where AfterHours does its thing. Usually a few F-bombs as well. People have taken Communion on bikes and in wheelchairs and, more times than you would think, with a dog in tow. Many times they will tell the person they are on the phone with, "Hold on, I gotta take Communion," and more than once I have had someone pass on Communion by saying, "I can't, Father, I'm drunk." This is where I have seen the gospel come to life more than any other place in my last seven years in ministry, probably in my life. Some people think we hand out peanut butter and jelly sandwiches. To us, it's having church.

Civic Center Park has often been noted as one of the central locations for drug dealing and prostitution in downtown Denver. The fact that it is at the corner of two major streets (Colfax and Broadway) makes for a lot of traffic, and that means customers. It is directly in front of the State Capitol and has a beautiful concrete amphitheater in its center that is stunning at first glance, unless you go into one of the small side alcoves that sit on either side of the stage and see someone shooting up. Then it's just ugly. (Seeing someone shooting up looks very different in real life than it does on TV or in the movies. In those mediums, it is strangely fascinating—the same way people slow down to see a train wreck. In real life, it just looks deeply, deeply sad.)

The park changed me from day one—long before I started doing church in a bar. As I like to say, first came the poor—then came the *pour*. I got ordained in June 2009. By July, I was passing out peanut butter and jelly sandwiches and Communion in the park. In the United Methodist tradition, you need to be an ordained elder in order to consecrate the elements of bread and juice. (In the UMC, we don't use wine. This works out well in the park, since so many of those on the street are fighting active addictions.) I started going to the park by myself with no intention that that first day would be the first of thousands of days I would hand out Communion to our city's least and lost. I also didn't envision ever stopping, so this sacrament quite naturally became part of AfterHours from the beginning. In August 2014, we did the math and realized we had passed out over 100,000 lunches in that park. One lunch at a time. Eyeball to eyeball. One person at a time.

I may have started alone, but it didn't stay that way. It wasn't long before I was sitting in a bar having beers with my buddy Ryan Canaday and a shift began. Ryan was the campus minister for the University of Denver Wesley Foundation, the United Methodist campus ministry. In no time at all, college students were knocking out fifty to a hundred lunches on Thursday nights. That's how AfterHours in the Park went from Jerry doing his weird, bat-shit crazy thing to a *whole bunch* of people doing it. I called it "the Table" early on. To myself, I still do. I like it.

From those days six years ago when I was taking fifty lunches down to the park by myself, we have grown. We now have groups taking lunches down to the park every day of the week, 365 days a year, rain or shine. People from our

Monday night gatherings come to hand out lunches they made. Some are corporate sponsors, some are little inner-city churches, some are big suburban churches. Some days, it is just a bunch of friends getting together, throwing a party, and knocking out a hundred lunches to feed a bunch of strangers. Day in, day out, week in, week out, we feed the city's poorest of the poor.

FRIENDS WITHOUT HOMES

It is an interesting scenario in the park. We go there intending to be Christ for those we serve. However, more times than not, it is *we* that see Christ in *them*. They have taught me grace and generosity, gratitude and straight up simple kindness. Are some of them drug addicts? Yep. Are some dealers and hookers and drunks? Check. Check. Check. Truth is, sometimes those on "our" side of the Communion and sandwich table battle addictions and other demons of all shapes and sizes too. Having a roof over your head is not the defining factor of whether you are a train wreck or not. I have served churches where the people are better dressed but just as much of a hot mess. We all have monkeys on our backs. Some are just more glaring. Others have gotten better at hiding behind fancy cars, nice clothes, and big houses. Having served a very affluent community in the suburbs, I realize that brokenness happens everywhere. I remember being in front of the congregation in the suburbs, looking out while preaching, and thinking, "Your son just got kicked out of school, and your husband is having an affair, and you're addicted to porn, and . . ." You just wouldn't know it because their Dockers were so well pressed and their hair was perfect. I get it—I lived in

Hollywood, the land where perception is reality. It is an easy game to be tempted to play; I have played it my whole life. I still do. We all do. The challenge is to constantly play it less and less.

It's different in the park. The folks in the park—our "friends without homes" as we call them, because that's all they really are—have the same problems. They just exert a lot less energy pretending they don't. It is like all that effort to put up a facade got too exhausting and they said, "Screw it. I'm a mess. Moving on." That is refreshing.

It is often so easy to lump the poor and homeless all together, as if there is a step-by-step instruction booklet on how to end up homeless. Step 1: Use up all your resources. Step 2: Develop an active addiction. Step 3: Become unemployable. Step 4: Lose your shit.

It simply doesn't work that way.

It's a complicated issue with many intersecting causes. And make no mistake—we are not under any impression that we are curing homelessness. We never intended to. Our goal is to treat the least and lost the way we believe Jesus would treat them: with kindness and compassion and love. We advocate with other groups to help end homelessness; we believe there are ways to solve this problem. But in the meantime, we give them a sandwich and love. City and local government have different goals and different agendas than we do. It is a beautiful thing when we can work together. But we are called to follow Jesus. This is actually pretty simple; it's just not easy.

Some folks have said in the past that groups like ours perpetuate homelessness, making people dependent on us. Maybe. I don't think so. There are very few homeless people I serve five days a week who would say, "Get off the street? And give up *this?* A brown paper bag filled with chips, a sandwich, and a granola bar? *Plus* bottled water? Why would I want to give *this* up?" I'm not trying to be a sarcastic ass (okay, maybe I am), but does anyone really think that the homeless stay homeless so they can eat peanut butter and jelly sandwiches? We aren't handing out rib eyes, people. On top of that, a number of the folks we feed *do* have a roof over their head and do have jobs. Or they are on disability. Here is my take: if you are willing to eat peanut butter and jelly seven days a week to help you get from payday to payday, AfterHours & Co. is there for you.

Being with and feeding the poor is the most fulfilling part of my job, hands down. And the *being with* part is crucial; this is not about throwing food at people. It is not a field trip in which we go down and feed the humans. It is about being in relationship with them. Yes, we get cold when it is 8 degrees in February, and it does kind of suck when it's 98 in August, but it is simple and clean. No bullshit. It cuts to the core of the biblical imperative to be with those on the margins. I always struggle with faith communities that say being with the poor isn't their *thing*. I think we are all different, and different churches emphasize different things. Depending on our context and the people we serve, it is going to look different for everybody. But Jesus did not make caring for the poor optional, and to see serving the poor as just a "spoke in the wheel" of being a Christian and a follower of Jesus? I have to call that bullshit.

I think it can look a million different ways, but the world has to see it. They have to *see* how we are changing the world for the better and see us living like J. C.

I believe that when they do, they will come running.

ANGELS AMONG YOU

This morning I had a bagel with cream cheese. It was awesome. I love bagels with cream cheese. Always have. A bagel is even better when you put butter on it and *then* the cream cheese. But a bagel is best when you put tuna on top of that, with mayo, butter, and cream cheese. I usually keep a defibrillator nearby just in case. When we run out of bagels with cream cheese, it is a very short time before we are back in ready supply.

The park has taught me how awesome I have it. More often than not, I can catch myself being a whiny little bitch, constantly looking around and seeing what I don't have. In "Come on up to the House," Tom Waits sings, "The only thing that you can see is all that you lack." That's me most of the time—unless I spend time with those who have less.

One time when some of the AfterHours folks were handing out food, we wound up with a few extra granola bars. Someone asked Dante, one of our friends without a home, if he wanted them. You would have thought he just won the lottery. After he took them, he was silent for a second and then said, barely loud enough for anyone to hear, "Wow, I can't remember the last time I had extra food."

How easy it is for us to take things for granted.

I am writing this at my kitchen table having my third Diet Coke of the morning, and I am within feet of hundreds and hundreds of dollars of food. Food in the cupboard, food in the fridge, food on top of the fridge, food we freeze because we have so much food that some of it would spoil before we are in the *mood* to eat it. I bet we have three kinds of crackers and at least that many kinds of pasta.

Food always tastes better after I have been in the park—and I always appreciate it more. The guys aren't saints. Some are hustlers, doing what they have to do to survive. But they help me see the world differently, maybe just a little more like God sees it.

Eddie's a good guy. At first glance, you would never guess he was homeless. He's clean-cut, soft-spoken, gentle, and polite. He has struggled with the bottle but has been sober for eighteen months.

One day he walked up to me and handed me a firecracker. He told me, "I want you to have this. I was gonna use it last night. I had a toy gun, and I was gonna put myself into a situation that would get the police called, light a few as they got there, and point the gun at them. They would take me out quick. That was my plan at least. But because of how much you guys have been down here, I started thinking about all of you. I couldn't do it. I want you to have this firecracker to remind you that you guys are making a difference."

It took everything for me to not completely lose it.

You never *ever* know the effect you are having on others. Make it be a good one. Things that you might not think twice about could change the course of people's lives. What we do and how we treat people matter—even when they're the littlest of things. Don't catch yourself thinking otherwise. Whether it's on the plains of Kansas, the inner city of Chicago, or the suburbs of Orlando, what we do matters, and I believe God is not only watching but counting on us.

When Tyrone started coming to us years ago, I don't even know if he had a job or a home. He now has both. He has had some challenges in the past with the law. He has been in the park to receive Communion and food before going on his way. Like many folks we feed in the park, he has a job, but these lunches help make ends meet. Tyrone is always decked out to the nines, and you can bet that his hat will match his pants and maybe his shoes. He is a gift and loves God with all his heart. He has written and memorized a number of poems. He is passionate about justice. He is a friend. Right after Christmas in the Park 2014, Tyrone sent me a Facebook message that said, "My time with you is done. My work is accomplished. Take care, Jerry. Working with you has been a joy and a gift. Always remember, you never know who are the angels among you."

After Tyrone was in the park with us four to five days a week every week for over a year, I never saw him again.

You never know.

A while back, a man and his son were in line. This is actually pretty rare. Even though families are the largest growing segment of the homeless population, most of the folks we deal with in the park are what is often referred to as chronically homeless. They are a lot of guys who look probably like the picture in your head: unkempt, dirty, dressed in old clothes, and in some cases, smelly. You know, the kingdom of God.

Anyway, this guy in front of the father and son got out of line, came over to me, pulled me aside, and said, "Hey man, are you cool if this guy and his son go to the front of the line? This kid shouldn't have to wait." I told him that I needed to check with the other guys in line. I asked them, "Hey all, are you cool if we let this guy and his son scoot up to the front?" Like Moses parting the Red Sea, these guys all silently took a step back and let the man and his boy walk by them to the front.

As they did, I heard one of the guys say to the man next to him, "That's a shame, man. That kid didn't ask to be homeless."

Few of them did. I rarely have been so proud of the guys.

The goal is to give the guys a little dignity, to make them feel a little less like a "them" and a little more like an "us." It is not to make them just like us.

It is also not charity. Charity is when you give while receiving nothing in return. The time in the park is, as they say in the courtroom, *quid pro quo*—this for that. The poor of our city save us. They save those of us who come to serve them from our greed, our self-centeredness, our arrogance, our self-absorption. They remind me not to bitch when I run out of Diet Coke. They remind me not to bitch when I can't find the shirt I am looking for because my closet is stuffed with *so many shirts* that it's hard to find a particular one. They remind me that while it sucks that we often don't have enough money from paycheck to paycheck and don't know how we will send our son to college let alone how we will ever retire, we are not trying to make $122 last a whole month. They give me perspective on this world and on my life.

Let me tell you about Cecil. Cecil is one of the first folks we met down in the park. He is a veteran and is faithful to his wife, who was a serious heroin addict when I met him. I asked him how he was doing, and he said, "Me? I'm doing great. We found a pallet that keeps us off the ground, and we got a tarp that we can connect to a dumpster. The dumpster blocks the wind, and the tarp keeps the rain off us. We are in an alley next to a pawnshop, so it is well lit and has security cameras, so we feel safe. Yeah, we are doing great. Some of these poor bastards have got it pretty rough, though."

Cecil lives in an alley next to a dumpster under a tarp, but he is doing great. I run out of angel hair pasta and have to eat penne, and I start bitching.

Good Lord. Who is teaching whom?

Mother Teresa supposedly said this about the United States: "I don't understand your country. In my country, we have people with one banana, and I have watched them split that banana to share it with someone else. In your country, you have people with entire *bunches* of bananas and won't give any away."

I've got to respectfully disagree. I have seen time and time again people in Civic Center Park open their lunches that they just received and split them with someone who came late to line and didn't get anything. It is stunning.

A number of our homeless guys now show up at our gatherings at the bars. They feel they can do so because they actually know a number of people when they get there. They recognize them from the park.

So now when Dan shows up at the Irish Rover, he isn't "homeless guy Dan." He's just Dan. And people shout out his name and call him to come over and sit with them. He sits and laughs and shares and takes it all in. He has been given a gift that's far more important than a peanut butter and jelly sandwich.

He has been given community.

It is an amazing thing to see members of our home-less community slip on plastic gloves, pull out some bread and jelly and peanut butter, and make sandwiches for other homeless people! Sometimes they will be in line the next day and will get the lunches they helped make the day before.

Community, responsibility, giving back—sounds like the kingdom of God to me.

SPIRITUAL FOOD

Feeding people physically and meeting their tangible, felt needs is essential. But we also have the opportunity to feed people's souls as well. Communion has always been special to me. I'm sure it has to do with my Catholic roots. I remember one time in my altar boy days when the priest was down a Communion server and told me I would be filling in. I remember thinking, "Isn't anyone more qualified? I'm eight." I did it, and I remember that I got to serve Communion to my mom and dad. I was hooked.

Communion connects with me in a special, kind of indescribable way. I can't explain it. Maybe that's why it's called "this holy mystery" in our liturgy. I like the words, the ritual, the ceremony, but especially the feeling. Communion has always been what Marcus Borg called "a thin place" for me—a place or moment when the stuff that lies between us and God is nearly translucent.

I believed that Communion could be that way for a lot of the guys in the park too.

Even believing that, I get surprised at how meaningful Communion can be for them. One time, I could see a guy running toward us from about fifty yards away. We had already given away all the lunches and most of the single sandwiches. All that was left was one sandwich in a baggie. I put it on the Communion table and waited for him. When he got close enough to shout, he said, "Are you guys done already?" I told him, "Dude, you lucked out. We got one PBJ left. It's yours." He looked at me with a bit of a confused expression and said, "Oh no, I've already eaten. Are you still doing Communion?"

Sometimes we think we know what people are hungry for, only to be surprised that it is their soul, not their body, that longs to be fed. (But someone else certainly needed that last sandwich.)

It still throws me when I ask someone if they would like Communion and they say, "What's that?" That is a moment. I try not to blow it. Even as I try, I realize that I don't know if I really *do* know what it is.

I try to break it down to its core: "This is a reminder of how much God loves you," I always say, whether someone is receiving the bread and juice for the first time or the hundredth. One day, when I served Eddie, one of our regulars, and said the same thing, he didn't miss a beat. He looked at me and said, "You guys are a reminder of how much God loves me."

It took everything I had to choke back the tears. Eddie reminded me of something we say every time we performed Communion when I was growing up in the church: "Pour out your Holy Spirit on these gifts and us gathered here. Make them be for us the body and blood of Christ *so that we may be the body of Christ in the world.* Help us be one with Christ, one with each other, and one in unity with all the world."

In a flash, I was reminded that it is not just the elements but *we* who are the body of Christ. We are the sacrament. We are the offering, freely given. God gave to us, and we give to others. The fancy church word for us becoming this sacrament is incarnation. We *become* Christ.

We live in a world where so many people are broken. The number one reason people tell me they don't want Communion is that they don't feel worthy. I always tell them that we are ready when they are ready, but what I want to say—no, scream—is, "You don't have to be worthy! That's the whole point! It's a gift, freely given! You don't have to earn it!" Maybe some day we will get the point across. It really seems that if there is one thing keeping us all from moving forward whenever we get stuck, it's the idea of grace. We understand forgiveness—kind of. Someone says they are sorry, and we forgive them—end of story. Grace is a whole other beast. Grace says, "I know you don't deserve to be forgiven. Hell, you ain't even asked to be forgiven.

You know what? You are forgiven anyway." We just can't grasp it. Maybe we believe it for some other people, just not for ourselves. We screwed it up way too big. Even God ain't gonna forgive this one.

I've seen this happen right in front of my eyes. I had never seen him before, nor have I seen him since. The man was maybe ten or twelve people back in line, but even from where I was standing, I could tell he had been crying. When he got up to me and I offered him Communion, he nodded yes. When I said, "This is a reminder of how much God loves you," he looked me in the eye and said, "Still?"

I told him yes, and he took Communion and went on down the line and disappeared.

It's hard to understand such total, unencumbered grace. It is so foreign, so out of our world, so different from our understanding, we simply can't believe it. I even have trouble with it myself sometimes.

There was one day when, through a series of mishaps, miscommunications, and simple logistics, we didn't get the lunches to the park. This has only happened about three or four times in the last six years, but I still felt like crap. People had been waiting, desperately needing food, and I let them down.

So the next day, I stood in front of the guys to apologize.

I said, "Guys, I understand the lunches didn't make it to you yesterday. There were lots of reasons, but excuses don't matter, I know that. I just want you to know that the buck stops with us. We fucked up. I wanted to look you in the eyes and say that and tell you I'm sorry."

One of the guys stepped out of the line, walked over to me, put his hand on my shoulder, shook my other hand, looked me dead in the eye, and said, "You're forgiven."

I almost lost it.

He had long brown hair and dark eyes and weather-beaten skin. It felt like Jesus himself forgave me. It felt like grace.

I know that may never happen again. I know the next time they may want to kick my ass. But everyone—everyone—should feel that kind of forgiveness once in their life. If we all forgave like that—like Jesus told us to—I think the world wouldn't be able to get to us fast enough.

We in the church often argue about some stupid things, things that the average nonchurchgoer couldn't care less about. They are usually theological things, and while they seem important to us, most "normal folks" just don't see the point. They want to know forgiveness. They want to know grace. And isn't that what it's all about?

I know we aren't changing homelessness. We are not changing the situation of the homeless people we encounter. But I also know that feeding our friends without homes is the least important thing we do down there in the park. At last check, there are more than thirty places where the city's homeless can get food throughout the week. Our food is the least of our "services offered."

The services we offer are simple. We offer dignity, we offer joy, we offer laughter, we offer hope and mercy and kindness in a place that doesn't see much of any of those. We are a group of people that comes together to serve strangers kindness and love.

ROLLING UP OUR SLEEVES

On a retreat this past year, I found myself in an interesting conversation. A colleague of mine who pastors a large church came up to me as we were walking out of a restaurant. He put his arm around me and said, 'Are you even going to be able to stand being with us for these couple of days? I mean, I know you think we are the ones who are doing it all wrong." The irony is that he was pastoring one of the largest churches in the conference and my little group of outsiders didn't even number fifty. It seemed odd for him to even make the comment. I am just a gnat to him.

I think I knew what he was getting at, though. After-Hours does church differently—really differently from a lot of churches. Many don't even call us a church. They call us a ministry. That cracks me up. I kind of like it because ministry connotes action. I think our emphasis is in a different place. It isn't on classes. It isn't on the music program—or any program for that matter. It isn't on the youth or children's ministry. It isn't on the building or the worship or the preaching. Everything we do is based around one question: Does this word/action/thought bring more love or less love into the world? In short, does it make us better disciples?

People want to help the poor, those in need, those who are struggling. I know this! I see it every week, every *day* in the park. People roll up their sleeves and open their wallets for things that help people in need. What people don't want to pay for is choir robes, or carpet, or million dollar parking lots. We want to pay for the stuff we think Jesus would have put his money toward. That would be the widow, the poor, and the orphan. It wouldn't be flat-screen TVs.

I know I can be judgmental of Christians who don't prioritize the poor. When I wasn't serving on a steady basis, I found I was a much more "live and let live" kind of person. I was more accepting, more open to letting people do their own thing. Looking back on that, I think it was my way of figuring that if I didn't judge others, they couldn't judge me. As I served more consistently, it was easy to get condescending. I was living a life of service, but I was more judgmental of those who weren't.

Clearly, the best of both worlds would be to serve others while remaining nonjudgmental of those living a life different from mine. I keep working at that. I'm pretty good at that when it's the guys in the park or a hipster skeptic trying out our gathering in the pub for the first time. I'm not so good when it's a Bible-thumping preacher saying the end is near.

Mary is from Missouri and was in Denver working for AmeriCorps. She first came to AfterHours in the park before coming to the bar because, as she told me, "I wanted to see if you were full of shit or not." Apparently we passed the test, because Mary started coming to both the park and the bars where we do our gathering. Mary had a mouth like mine (not good) and a heart even bigger than Mother Teresa's (very good). She was exactly who I designed AfterHours for. One time I asked about her religious background. She had an undergraduate degree in religion. I asked her if she had been raised in the church. She said, "My dad is a Southern Baptist pastor." I just stared at her. She did not look, act, smell, or talk like a preacher's kid. When I realized I was just staring at her, she said, "Yeah, we don't talk about it." I had to imagine those dinner conversations were awkward at best.

One morning before going to the park, I got a text from Mary saying that her dad was visiting and she would be bringing him to the park to help hand out food and socks and Communion.

As soon as I read this, I got judgmental. What is this guy going to say to the group of my favorite junkies, prostitutes, dealers, and ex-cons that make up our daily line? I had visions of him damning them to hell unless they repented and trying to perform miracle healings of their afflictions. Yeah, I know. I suck.

We put Mary's dad in charge of handing out socks at the end of the line. It's pretty easy and something great for a first-timer to do because, well, handing someone a pair of socks isn't brain surgery. I kept one eye on the Communion elements and one eye on him, watching to see if he would try to perform a rogue baptism in the park or damn some-one to the depths of hell. I didn't know how they operated. The only Southern Baptists I knew were either on TV or members of my family on my mom's side down in Abilene, Texas. I have heard those Baptists could be a sneaky bunch.

To my surprise, Mary's dad was compassionate and gracious and full of kind words. He looked right at home handing out socks and chatting with the guys, hearing their stories, and listening more than talking. I felt like a total ass. The one thing people will nail the conservative right for is how quick they are to judge, and here I was doing the same thing in spades.

Mary later told me that when her dad got back to his church in Missouri, he couldn't shut up about the work he had seen in the park: how he had seen the Holy Spirit at work changing lives, how he had seen Christ's mercy lived out in a tangible, real way; he kept going on and on. Eventually, the leaders at his church said, "Pastor, if you were so moved by their work, why don't we support what they are doing?" From that moment on, they wrote a check every month to pay for socks that we hand out in the park. Every month.

This blew my mind. That a small, conservative Southern Baptist church in Missouri would be willing to support an urban progressive church in a bar that catered to dealers and hookers and homeless was almost more than my heart could take. And when Mary's dad's church closed after a natural disaster, they found themselves in a quandary: how to spend an insurance settlement when they were not rebuilding. They found a way by donating a large chunk of it to AfterHours. I felt like the Grinch whose heart grew three sizes that day—plus two.

I learned a lot from that. I learned not to box people in by their religion. I learned that a progressive liberal pastor could be as big a judgmental idiot as a conservative right-leaning preacher can be. I learned that grace and compassion and kindness come in all shapes and sizes. I also learned that when we get down to the core of the gospel—love one another as I have loved you—we have a lot more in common than our differences would suggest. Regardless of your politics or geography or theology, everyone wants to be part of something that makes a difference.

This is why I think AfterHours works. I don't think it is because we do church in a bar. So what? If that was our only thing, we would just look like another hipster bar church trying to be cool. We feed the poor first and foremost because caring for those on the margins seems to be a primary concern for Jesus, and if it is a primary concern for Jesus, than it should be a primary concern for us. People want to help others, and nothing motivates people to roll up their sleeves more than seeing priests and ministers and preachers and pastors rolling up *their* sleeves. On top of that, it reminds me that not only am I trying to help others be better followers of Jesus, but I am trying to be one too! Lugging water to the park to feed the poor on a 98-degree day reminds me that I ain't all that. It keeps me humble (okay, who's kidding whom—maybe not *humble,* but in the ballpark, or near the ballpark). Half of the homeless guys didn't even know I was clergy for the first two years I was in the park, and that's okay. My doing it got others doing it.

When I was a bartender, the best thing a manager could do was to help out. When I was buried and in the weeds, with three deep at the bar, when a manager would roll up his or her sleeves and wash glassware, or run food, or go in back and get beer and restock the beer fridge, that was awesome. When managers would do that, I would fall on the sword for them! They showed me they weren't too good to put in the work and get their hands dirty.

I have been called a sanctimonious ass for talking about AfterHours' work with the homeless. "Holier than thou" stings like a bitch. But I don't serve because I am holy. I serve because I feel most on purpose, most alive, and most like I am following Jesus when I am in the park with our city's homeless. I feel like I am not just going through the motions when I am with them. I feel like what we do matters and that we are making the world a better place when we serve those with less.

Conclusion

ALWAYS AN EMCEE

I thought I made a huge career change at forty. I moved my family across the country to go 180 degrees away from entertainment, which I knew so well, into the uncharted waters of ministry, of which I knew *nothing*. I thought I was making an enormous switch from one side of the career spectrum to the other. After all, one rarely sees those two careers mentioned side by side: L.A. comic and organized religion—unless the comic is making fun of the organized religion.

What I have come to figure out is that while the venues and the audiences have changed, my job description has stayed the same.

There's a scene in *Taken* with Liam Neeson where he is talking on the phone with the kidnappers who have just taken his daughter and he is explaining who he is. He says something along the lines of, "I have a very specific set of skills, skills that I have acquired over a very long career."

I feel like Liam Neeson sometimes (with better hair but more body fat), because I also have a very specific set of skills that I have acquired over a very long career. My specific set of skills involves creating joy. I have done corporate picnics, warmed up studio audiences, hosted giveaways, DJed at nightclubs and at weddings and bar mitzvahs, and generally been the guy brought in to "bring the happy."

I have in front of me my biggest challenge to date: make church fun. I take very seriously the instruction that I mentioned earlier in Nehemiah 8:10: "Then he said to them, 'Go your way, eat the fat and drink sweet wine and send portions of them to those for whom nothing is prepared, for this day is holy to our LORD; and do not be grieved, for the joy of the LORD is your strength.'"

Some won't take AfterHours seriously, and that's okay. We need all kinds. But it's because of that verse that I know years of hosting Hula Hoop contests really can pay off for the kingdom!

My career has changed, but my ministry has remained the same. I have really held one job and done one thing since I was twenty-one. Whether I am hosting an IMAX show for a thousand people twelve times a day, leading people in karaoke in a supermarket, writing a theme-park show that I will never see, bartending at a pool hall, being a mall Santa, handing out sandwiches to the homeless, leading a theology pub, or giving a sermon, I am just an emcee. I create joy.

I believe that joy is a vehicle for producing change. Laughter is one of those changes, but it doesn't stop there. Joy is addicting. People want more of it when they get it. Joy is like a drug.

And I'm a dealer.

I used to say, "Ladies and gentlemen, Jay Leno." Now I am the opening act for God. My job has always been to bring more joy into people's lives. The only thing that has changed is the venues and who's headlining.

I have never been the main event. Never.

I hosted picnic games for lawyers every summer in Malibu. Four hundred lawyers and their families with no amplification—I would lose my voice every Monday.

I was a DJ at a nightclub where I would lead everyone in paper airplane tosses, Hula Hoop contests, and "Name

That Tune" between the band's sets. Five nights a week, I gave away T-shirts—the glamorous life of the entertainer.

I was the house emcee at the most famous comedy club in the world, bringing up the biggest stars of stand-up and television: Jerry Seinfeld, Drew Carey, Adam Sandler, David Spade, Sam Kinison, and Jay Leno.

The one thing they all had in common was that nobody in those audiences knew who I was. No one cared. My job was to get people excited about the main event. The main event could have been a band they came to see, a comic they had heard about, or the buffet at the company picnic. The one thing I knew for sure? They weren't coming to see me.

Maybe that was good training. Should churchgoers go to see the preacher, pastor, or priest? Should they go to enjoy the one introducing the main act or the main act itself? Worship leaders should be like the finger pointing to the moon. No one should be looking at the finger. They should be trying to find the moon.

I'm an emcee for God. The emcee's job is to get the audience ready for the headliner, to interact with them, to prepare them for their interaction with the one they came to see. What the emcee can never do is begin to think that the audience is there to see them. That kind of thinking can get you fired in a hurry. Know that your job is to serve the person that the people came to see. When you forget that, your ego gets out of whack and you forget why you are there in the first place.

I have created joy and will continue to do so— through a sandwich, a joke, a story, or a kind word. In a nutshell; I'm just trying to put more love in the world and help others do the same.

Preparing the way for the headliner. *That's* a show you don't wanna miss . . .

CPSIA information can be obtained
at www.ICGtesting.com
Printed in the USA
LVOW01s0316281015

459814LV00003B/4/P